Problem Solving for Healthcare Workers

How to Get Better – Lessons Can Be Learned

Problem Solving for Healthcare Workers

How to Get Better – Lessons Can Be Learned

By
John Michael Collins

CRC Press
Taylor & Francis Group
Boca Raton London New York

CRC Press is an imprint of the
Taylor & Francis Group, an **informa** business

A PRODUCTIVITY PRESS BOOK

CRC Press
Taylor & Francis Group
6000 Broken Sound Parkway NW, Suite 300
Boca Raton, FL 33487-2742

© 2018 by John Michael Collins
CRC Press is an imprint of Taylor & Francis Group, an Informa business

No claim to original U.S. Government works

Printed on acid-free paper

International Standard Book Number-13: 978-1-138-30582-3 (Paperback)
International Standard Book Number-13: 978-1-138-30586-1 (Hardback)
International Standard Book Number-13: 978-0-203-72872-7 (eBook)

Library of Congress Cataloging-in-Publication Data

Names: Collins, John Michael, 1940- author.
Title: Problem solving for healthcare workers : how to get better - lessons can be learned / John Michael Collins.
Description: Boca Raton : Taylor & Francis, 2018. | Includes bibliographical references.
Identifiers: LCCN 2017032935| ISBN 9781138305823 (paperback : alk. paper) | ISBN 9781138305861 (hardback : alk. paper) | ISBN 9780203728727 (ebook)
Subjects: LCSH: Medical care--Quality control.
Classification: LCC RA399.A1 C65 2018 | DDC 362.1--dc23
LC record available at https://lccn.loc.gov/2017032935

Visit the Taylor & Francis Web site at
http://www.taylorandfrancis.com

and the CRC Press Web site at
http://www.crcpress.com

To all healthcare workers, wishing them every success in their work.

Contents

Foreword

Following a number of high-profile examples of failures in the British National Health Service (NHS) over the last decade, patient safety is reaching the top of the healthcare agenda. The Francis Inquiry report clearly identified that the responsibility for ensuring quality of care sits within board rooms and senior management teams. While this gives patients the profile and scrutiny they so rightly deserve, it has to be the business of everyone working in healthcare, and 'doing no harm' should be at the forefront of the minds of all healthcare professionals.

The majority of healthcare practitioners work tirelessly to provide the best possible care for their patients. Providing front-line care in the face of increasing demands, limited resources *and* financial constraints undoubtedly places a strain on those delivering care – but by keeping patients at the heart of services, it is possible to achieve better quality care as well as cost savings.

It is easy to be led into thinking that errors are happening all the time; however, every day more than a million people are treated safely and successfully in the NHS, and thankfully, errors are extremely rare. Regardless, NHS patients have the right to expect to be treated safely and be protected from avoidable harm.

Advances in technology and knowledge in recent decades, however, have created an immensely complex healthcare system. This complexity brings new risk, and evidence shows that things will – and do – go wrong in the NHS; patients are sometimes harmed no matter how dedicated and professional the staff are. When errors do occur, they can have catastrophic outcomes for both patients and practitioners alike. Errors are seldom purely the fault of individuals and are usually the result of problems of the systems they work in.

There is a need for radical change in both culture and environment in the NHS, and we must look towards more patient-orientated healthcare. Donald M. Berwick (former president and chief executive officer [CEO] of the Institute for Healthcare Improvement) stated that 'The real challenge for the NHS is to shift the culture of command and control to one in which staff are engaged in decision-making and fulfil their potential as one of the greatest sources of ideas for innovation and learning'.

One way of realising this is through improved education and training for the clinicians delivering care on the front line. This training needs to focus not only on *why* continuous improvement is important, but also on *how* to integrate this into everyday practice, making it feel part of normal care, just like delivering evidence-based clinical care. This ideally needs to be instilled into clinical training at an early stage. Clinicians work in a multitude of different settings, and whether they are in or out of hospitals or working with other professionals and agencies to deliver complex care across health and social care, we need to foster the culture that patient safety is everyone's responsibility.

This book presents a practical and refreshing approach to patient safety and continuous improvement in patient care. It will help practitioners reflect on how they can remove the obstacles that sometimes prevent them from doing what they want to do: deliver high-quality and safe patient care. It has helpful tools and practical applications for individuals and teams to enable them to work together to review their services and to identify where root problems might exist.

It is a must-read for both pre- and post-registered healthcare professionals and managers alike, and if put into practice, it could go some way towards bringing about the crucial shift in mindset and thus create an empowered and aligned clinical workforce.

Monica Fletcher, OBE

Preface

What This Book Is About

While the UK NHS has an extremely high success rate at the most challenging lifesaving work, and we all know of friends and relatives who have had supreme care in the most serious of circumstances, there are still occasions where mistakes are made and patients' lives have been put at risk and lost.

My motivation for writing this book started shortly after 2007 when stories of appalling care standards at the Mid Staffordshire NHS Trust came to public notice. These were confirmed in 2013 when Sir Robert Francis produced the findings of a public inquiry he had chaired.[1] The *Guardian* (Denis Campbell, 6 February 2013)[2] reported that 'a disputed estimate suggested that between 400 and 1200 patients had died at Stafford Hospital as a result of poor care between January 2005 and March 2009'. Whatever the actual numbers were (and no one will ever know), it was a very unsatisfactory situation.

The *Guardian* also reported that it might never have come to general notice without the tireless work of Julie Bailey who, when her mother died of poor care aged 86 in 2007, discovered other families with similar stories. They formed a campaign group and demanded a public inquiry. At the same time, the Healthcare Commission had noticed unusually high death rates at that trust, and as a result a number of inquiries took place, of which the Francis Report was the most damning. This is described more in Chapter 2.

Equally concerning is the continuing occurrence of baby deaths. Two years after the Kirkup Report[3] into the maternity departments of the Morecambe Bay Trust, when 3 mothers and 16 babies are believed to have died unnecessarily, reports from more hospitals are appearing in the media, one in Shrewsbury[4] where there were 7 suspicious deaths and another in Chester[5] after 15 babies' deaths were unexplained.

That is the down side, and there is a stark contrast between the best and the worst. If the Mid Staffordshire Trust was the worst in recent years then I would like to put these events into perspective, as it would be very unfair just to look at the negative aspects of healthcare in Britain.

So, to counterbalance these horror stories and illustrate the contrast in care standards, I need to report the events of 7 July 2005 and 22 March and 22 May 2017 and the wonderful responses of the emergency services to those terrorist attacks in London and Manchester.

I have chosen to mention the incident in London in July 2005 because it was before the reporting of poor care at Stafford. In London, two bomb attacks, one in the Underground and one on a London bus, killed over 56 people and injured 784. Although one close hospital, Great Ormond Street, did not have an accident and emergency department, the canteen was transformed into a field hospital with triage and 10 emergency beds, while the in-house branch of Costa Coffee was turned into a minor injuries unit.

University College London Hospital had implemented a major incident plan within an hour, hundreds of staff were called in and 70 casualties were treated.

The London Ambulance Service treated over 400 patients and learned many important lessons from the event.

So while in London in 2005 the emergency services responded supremely well to a major incident, at the same time only 160 miles away in Stafford, poor care was slowly killing hundreds. What a contrast.

The latest example of wonderful response in an emergency has happened while I have been finishing this book. On 24 May 2017, I watched the television reports unfold following a suicide bomb attack on the mostly young people at a pop concert in Manchester. At 10:30 in the evening the bomber killed 22 and injured 59 more. In a very short time, through well-rehearsed regional training, all of the emergency services were prepared for this major disaster, and 60 ambulances had been pulled in from about a 100-mile radius of stations. They transported the casualties to eight major trauma hospitals in the Manchester area. Off-duty staff heard the news and volunteered to come in to work, sometimes unpaid. Shift patterns were voluntarily exchanged between workers to make sure everything was covered. Where designated ambulances had been transferred closer to Manchester from the hinterland, other ambulances from further away were brought nearer to cover the gaps created.

More recently, on 20 June 2017, I watched a TV programme about the service provided by St Mary's Hospital Paddington to treat the victims of a terror attack on Westminster Bridge on 22 March 2017. By sheer chance, BBC2 had a filming unit in the accident and emergency department when the emergency was declared. The response I watched was incredibly magnificent. I cannot find other words to describe it.

These were outstanding examples of a world-class service achieved through good leadership, rehearsals, training and dedication.

This handbook is less appropriate for those healthcare professionals just mentioned, those on the front line or those doing ground-breaking work in other areas, but more appropriate for the hundreds of thousands of healthcare workers who are never likely to be in the limelight, but who perform a vital, routine job, day after day, often under difficult circumstances.

How often have we heard politicians say after some disastrous report, 'Lessons must be learned', but what does this really mean? Will responsible parties carry out a careful cause and effect analysis and methodically get to the root causes of the problem? Will sufficient steps be taken to permanently eradicate those causes and provide a permanent solution so that the problem will not reoccur? This is what is done in the aviation industry, with the result that air travel is very safe.

One recent comparison between safety in the aviation industry and in medicine has been reported by Stepheny Nebehay of Reuters[6]; it was made by the World Health Organisation (WHO) Envoy for Patient Safety, Professor Sir Liam Donaldson. When he was appointed in 2011, Professor Donaldson said, 'If you were admitted to hospital tomorrow in any country your chances of being subjected to an error in your care would be something like 1 in 10. Your chances of dying due to an error in healthcare would be 1 in 300. This compares with the risk of dying in an air crash of about 1 in 10 million passengers'.

This low accident rate in aviation is achieved by studying the causes and by using the methods of continuous improvement explained in this book. These methods are now becoming better known within British healthcare having been recommended in many recent UK government reports discussed in Chapter 2, but they are perhaps still misunderstood at grassroots healthcare levels.

Britain is not unique in being concerned about patient safety – in one study of deaths from preventable adverse events (PAEs) in the United States, John James estimated that there are at least 210,000 PAEs per annum.[7]

Another study by Martin Makary and Michael Daniel, published in the *British Medical Journal* (BMJ),[8] asserted that medical error was the leading cause of death in the United States.

While there is a great deal of research being carried out in the United Kingdom at a national level into such topics as 'never events', 'stillbirths', and 'causes of patient harm', described in Chapter 3, it takes time for conclusions to filter through to the workplace. I hope this book will help to create a demand for information from the grassroots/front-line levels of the organisation upwards to senior management.

Having experienced the NHS since its inception in 1948 and then moved into the professional aspects of industrial and commercial quality assurance, I have seen great changes in the ways healthcare has been delivered. Recently, in carrying out research for this book, I have gathered a wealth of accurate anecdotes, mostly negative, from very reliable sources that must remain anonymous. I have then weighed these anecdotes against what I would expect any organisation offering first-class customer service to have delivered to me, as a customer, and my conclusions show there are many 'lessons to be learned'.

The book is therefore my own quality specialist's view of quality in healthcare based on 30 years of industrial quality assurance experience. It includes my own assessment of the errors quoted in published, high-profile reports on TV, in the popular press, on the Internet and in recent government reports. As an outsider to the NHS, I can take an unbiased observer's view of the current situation.

The Aims

The aims of this handbook are to

1. Explain what continuous improvement is and why it is needed
2. Introduce the reader to the disciplined and structured problem-solving process, explaining how to keep auditable records to demonstrate that continuous improvement is being applied
3. Explain how individual teams in any healthcare setting can easily introduce continuous improvement
4. Help readers recognise quality control methods in their own workplace and understand how to contribute to existing continuous improvement activities

5. Help those who wish to introduce their own simple continuous improvement projects by providing some of the skills needed
6. Help any organisation that has had an adverse report at an audit or inspection, such as by the UK Care Quality Commission (CQC), to make the necessary improvements and achieve the appropriate standards
7. Help with the overall awareness and understanding of quality improvement and prepare readers to understand the principles behind the more advanced papers published by NHS England and others.

The book is a basic-level manual for those who have never been involved in any form of quality improvement and is also suitable as a refresher for anyone wishing to refamiliarise themselves with the various techniques discussed.

It does not tell the professional healthcare worker how to do their job – that is their business. Nor is it an academic treatise. It is simply a practical 'How to' guide for anyone wanting to make improvements where they work. The jargon has been kept to a minimum and the text made as readable as possible.

The Reader

The book has been written for anyone delivering healthcare, anyone responsible for the functioning of a health practice and/or patient outcomes and anyone chosen to work on a continuous improvement team, whether non-manager, manager or director. The target reader will probably not have read any UK government reports or the UK National Institute for Health and Care Excellence (NICE) guidelines from cover to cover but would like to have these specialist techniques explained and put into perspective.

Additionally, this book will be of special importance to anyone in a team, section or organisation that needs to make improvements following an audit or inspection.

Context

It is not a manual on statistics or quality control, but what it does that many papers or websites do not do is to put these methods into the context of everyday problem solving and continuous improvement.

Disclaimer

Whilst I have taken all due care to check the National Health Service statistics and the Internet references at the time of writing, because of the volatility of both, I cannot guarantee the data to be entirely accurate nor the references to be relevant after publication.

The Author

John Michael (Mike) Collins, MSc is an industrial technologist and a past fellow of the Institute of Quality Assurance, who has spent 30 years advising businesses to make improvements in quality, customer service and overall efficiency.

He advised many blue-chip companies and national corporations on the application of sound quality principles while working as a management consultant with Price Waterhouse, now known as PricewaterhouseCoopers, or PWC.

In his time as a management consultant he has shown a large number of businesses how to achieve certification to the relevant Quality System Standard. He has also helped many large organisations implement total quality continuous improvement programmes.

He has not worked in the NHS, so he brings an outsider's view of how improvements can be made, based on experiences within both large and small organisations across many business sectors.

Acknowledgements

In the spring of 2016, I had presentation copies of a draft version printed, bound and sent to a range of medical professionals for comment. One of those who has given me the most encouragement has been Monica Fletcher OBE, CEO of the charity Education for Health in Warwick. I was delighted when I received an extremely encouraging response from Monica, who had taken the time to go through the manuscript, cover to cover, to give me her personal critique on just about every aspect. She gave me the final motivation by telling me that in her opinion the book should be a standard text for all medical training courses. This was a real booster; thank you, Monica.

I must also thank Professor Lord Darzi, PC, KBE, the Paul Hamlyn Chair of Surgery at Imperial College London. After seeing the draft, he said, 'It was wonderful to receive your book, and as you rightly considered, anything about Quality Improvement in the NHS was bound to spark my interest! There cannot be enough said regarding the importance of effective QI implementation in the NHS so please do keep up the good work'. Thank you, Professor Darzi.

Dr. Bill Kirkup CBE, chairman of the Morecambe Bay investigation in July 2013, was very helpful, giving me advice on some of the competition the book would face.

During the publication process I have received superb guidance from Kristine Mednansky and Alexandria Gryder of Taylor & Francis, along with Lara Silva McDonnell at Deanta Global, to whom I give my thanks.

Thanks must also go to numerous friends who have offered encouragement and advice, Guy Garfit of the Large Print Bookshop, ex Longman Publishing; Adrian Thorpe, Richard Brook, Paul Smith and Jean Knowles.

Finally, overriding thanks go to my family, my sons and their wives and especially my wife Pauline, who have all been very supportive.

Prologue: Jennifer's Tale

This is the true story of a mother of two grown-up children, in her 40s, in Britain, that started in 2010 and did not finish until 2017. I have interviewed her several times since 2010 because she had a story then that was relevant to the book I was planning to write. Recent events have made the story even more relevant to the points I am making, and hence they form a prologue. At the end of the book there is an epilogue putting her story and the points I am making in this book into perspective.

This woman, Jennifer, is intelligent and alert and able to look after herself, thankfully, but during the two episodes described in this story she had periods of confusion, puzzlement, incredulity, disgust, pain, fear and worry when she should not have had. Looking back, she wonders, justifiably, what might have happened if she had not been able to manage herself while in hospital, that is, like the mythical sick little old man or lady?

In 2010, she was diagnosed as needing a hysterectomy and was admitted for the operation. The hysterectomy was carried out, but during the process an anti-clotting drug was given at the wrong time. This led to internal bleeding, and a second operation was needed at 8:30 p.m. on a Friday evening to remove the haematoma. I believe the day and time indicate the seriousness of her condition. This was when it was found that her bowel had been nicked by the first surgeon. Following the second operation she was given food when she should not have been, when a nasal stomach drain was in place, and the combined effect of these two errors caused her bowel to remain inactive for many days longer than normal.

These errors probably had a significant effect on her life for the following six years and maybe longer.

Eventually Jennifer was discharged, but she continued to suffer from abdominal pains which were attributed to irritable bowel syndrome (IBS) and were not investigated further.

Then, five years later she started to suffer from continual diarrhoea. Blood tests indicated there was no infection. The diarrhoea continued for another two weeks, when she started to also vomit bile. In this period, she was not eating and had lost weight, down to 6 stone 7 lb. Her general practitioner (GP) told her to go immediately to the local accident and emergency (A&E). It was 8:00 p.m. on a Thursday evening, and after a long wait in considerable pain Jennifer was seen at 1:00 a.m. on Friday. The registrar suspected bowel adhesions. A computed tomography (CT) scan was recommended, but the scanner was not available and there were no beds available so she was sent home in pain. (Jennifer learned many weeks later that both an x-ray and a CT scanner would have been available.)

Over the following weekend the pain continued, and on Monday she saw her GP who assessed her and tested her urine which revealed high ketones, sugar and high protein, indicating she was severely dehydrated; that sounded the alarm bells. The GP phoned the surgical team at the hospital and wrote a letter requesting she had immediate admission for treatment. She made her own way to A&E, but despite the GP's letter she had to go through triage and wait longer in considerable pain, losing consciousness at one stage. An x-ray was carried out, and she was found to have a bowel obstruction. She was then admitted to a well-run ward and was looked after very well pre-operation. *The x-ray on Monday showed the obstruction clearly enough to know that was the source of the problem, so why did the A&E doctor not do it early on the Friday morning, when it would have been possible?*

On admission for her bowel operation, Jennifer was asked about her allergies, and because she had in the past shown a reaction to a particular medication, she was given a printed red wrist band stating her personal details, and red, indicating an allergy. At several times during her operation and treatment, mostly when she was either in pain, tired or drugged, she was asked what the allergy was. This seemed strange to her, because how could what she said be relied upon when she was in that state of mind? *The obvious action was for the facts to be printed on the wrist band, so they would be indisputable. It seemed so logical and obvious to Jennifer that she was astounded that it was not done that way.*

She was then transferred to another ward at 6:30 p.m. where some of the nurses were rude and offhand, ignoring her requests for assistance; although observations had been requested, these were not carried out until 1:00 the following morning (6.5 hours later). Were these observations important? If so, why were they not carried out? *One can only conclude the reason was overwork and/or poor supervision.*

Prior to her operation, the anaesthetists decided that rather than giving Jennifer an epidural for pain relief they would use two cannulae to inject the pain killer, one in each side of her abdomen. Each had to be topped up at 12-hour intervals by a qualified anaesthetist.

While recovering in the ward two avoidable events interfered with this pain relief, causing Jennifer great discomfort for many hours.

On one occasion, when a 12-hour top up was required, the anaesthetist was attending to an emergency and was unable to attend to Jennifer, she just had to wait. *As this was a scheduled treatment, why could it not have been programmed into a timed programme for anyone who was qualified? Was this the only anaesthetist available? Did it really need an anaesthetist to do this?*

On the other occasion, one of the cannulae was leaking and one doctor believed that a top up could not be done until the leak was repaired, whereas another doctor was prepared to do it. There was a waste of time, and Jennifer was in pain for longer than was necessary. *Why did the cannula leak, and could it not have been replaced as soon as the leak appeared?*

That Wednesday at 8:00 p.m., she was operated on in a procedure lasting four hours; we need to call this Day 1. There was an obstruction, adhesions and a perforation; 40 cm of bowel were removed, and the wound required 25 staples. This was six days after first reporting to A&E the previous Thursday, and five weeks after first having diarrhoea. *The question must be asked why it took so long to take the necessary action – a delay that could have seriously affected her chances of survival.*

During her recovery on a ward of very variable care standards, various puzzling events took place that did not help the recovery process. On one day she went to the toilet with a rechargeable battery powered drip stand, but on her return to her bed the power for the drips was not plugged back into mains and eventually the drip failed. *Was this just a careless oversight?*

Shortly after the operation her catheter was removed by a nurse on the nurse's own initiative, but it should not have been, and the patient had to plead to have it re-instated. This was done, but only after an ultrasound scan had shown how full her bladder was; and of course it had to be replaced with difficulty. This was very distressing for her. *Was this a mistake or lack of care and attention?*

Jennifer was being fed through a cannula in her neck, this became infected and had to be removed. Another cannula in her arm also became infected, causing a very painful lump. These are both minor events in the grander scheme of things, but not if, like the patient, you have been seriously ill for six weeks. It is distressing and does not aid recovery. *Should it have been like that?*

While recovering, two incidents occurred that caused Jennifer severe alarm. One afternoon an unstable female patient, without warning, went up to the adjacent patient's bed and violently pushed the bed-tray towards that patient who was sitting in a chair. The contents of the tray, a drink and so on, were scattered around over the patient, who took the incident very calmly. The other patients were more vociferous, fearing what might happen to them. The nurses quickly took control, putting the unstable patient back to bed.

When Jennifer's husband arrived at visiting time, he asked what had happened and was told that the unstable patient had been sedated. Perhaps so, but some hours later that patient came out from behind the curtains and started to walk around again. All the other patients, including Jennifer, were severely alarmed again, given that they were all in post-operative recovery, fearing something similar might happen again. Why was this second disturbance allowed to happen? *Was it due to an inadequate assessment of the patient's condition and/or the lack of a secure room to quarantine that patient?*

But that was not the only frightening moment. A day or two later, at 1:00 a.m., Jennifer awoke to see a male patient from the adjacent male bay, standing at the end of her bed. This scared her, as she saw the man as a threat, especially when she had three tubes going into her and one tube coming out, all attached to stands, preventing her from moving away. *Again, why was this allowed to happen? Was it complacency?*

Jennifer was discharged on the Tuesday, 13 days after her operation. She knew that during the bowel resection a tissue sample of the blockage had been submitted to the pathology lab for testing, and she asked her GP about the results, but he had not received any report at all from the hospital. As the patient pointed out at the time, what if a complication had occurred and she had to visit the GP? He would not have known what the details of treatment had been, other than what she could tell him.

Desperate to receive some official story about her condition, Jennifer contacted her GP and, after making inquiries, the GP received the lab report which he forwarded to his patient. It was 52 lines long with five question marks against words such as 'unusual', 'adhesion', 'fistula', 'Crohn's disease', 'serosal adhesions', 'ischaemic change', 'probable gluten enteropathy', 'serological investigation recommended'. There was no summary or overview. The questions that sprang to mind were 'So what?', and 'What next?', 'Is that good or bad?' Later Jennifer's surgeon admitted he, too, was not sure what point the pathologist was making in the lab report.

The timescales of the document trail for the pathology were interesting. The sample was collected from theatre at midnight on Day 1, received by the lab on Day 2 at 10:08 a.m., the results reported on Day 16 at 10:17 a.m., sent to GP on Day 24 at 09:15 a.m. As of Day 24, neither the patient nor the GP knew the official interpretation or explanation of the laboratory test results. *Was this overwork, bad organisation or poor supervision?*

Inquiries with the consultant surgeon's secretary on Day 19 indicated that the patient's notes were still on the ward. Jennifer was disgusted at the lack of communication on what, to her, was such an important matter. Eventually the notes were located.

One of the findings of Jennifer's pathology test results was a query by the pathologist regarding 'gluten enteropathy' – did she have coeliac disease? The surgeon recommended that the GP should organise a blood test, which he did, about five weeks after the bowel operation. On attending for the blood test, the nurse was uncertain as to what tests to request from the pathology lab, because there was no definitive request for any specific test, and to her credit she Googled 'tests for gluten enteropathy'. *Why did she have to resort to Google?*

Then, when the nurse started to enter the blood test onto the pathology lab system, a warning flashed on the screen to say that the particular test had been done several weeks before the operation and gave a negative result. *So Jennifer had a wasted journey, the nurse wasted an hour or so, the consultant and the GP had wasted time and energy thinking about it, all because the system somehow let them down.*

Overview

Is this story exceptional or is it what we can come to expect in an overworked National Health Service (NHS)? I believe that the best of the NHS is world beating; but there are pockets where, through poor direction, poor management and perhaps local and national politics, standards are not as good as they should be.

To rationalise this story, look at it from two angles. First, on the one hand, if during a course of treatment, everything goes to plan, then a few minor irritations can be tolerated and are probably ignored. If, on the other hand, when the main purpose is either not achieved or only achieved with difficulty, then minor irritations will blow up out of proportion and will not be ignored. Indeed, having experienced serious problems, most patients will be watching out for mistakes and will become acute observers.

Jennifer's tale also illustrates another very important fact, only the patient sees the full journey from primary care through to secondary care and back again. Each professional only sees their own small involvement, as if through a knothole in a piece of wood. The treatment is a chain of events, each link in the chain relying on good records and communication from the previous ones to ensure the best results.

The other angle is rather like a driving test. If during the test the learner driver does not make any errors serious enough to fail but makes many minor mistakes, the examiner will judge that the learner is not capable enough to be allowed to drive unsupervised and will fail the learner.

Are we expecting too much not to be annoyed, irritated or confused when we are at our most vulnerable state; are we just being unrealistic perfectionists?

How many minor irritations experienced during a hospital visit are needed to constitute a failure and be a serious cause for concern? In Jennifer's case, there appeared to be too many irritations to have confidence in the hospital where she was treated.

Can lessons be learned? I hope so.

Chapter 1

How Lessons Are Learned

SUMMARY

To learn lessons from mistakes, those in authority at an appropriate management level have to answer 11 questions. If they do not, the lessons will be forgotten. Complacency must be avoided, because a low tolerance towards minor errors will help to reduce major ones. Disasters are often an accumulation of several minor errors.

'Lessons must be learned' is the common expression usually coming after some disastrous event involving a serious mishap, an unfortunate chain of events or the discovery of serious maladministration. If the unfortunate event has been serious enough it will have hit the headlines and received attention at a high level. However, by the time it has hit the headlines it is really too late – all the normal controls that should have worked will have failed, and the situation will be in quality failure mode. Where good quality assurance systems are in place, there will be well-established routines to follow. This book will guide the reader through some of these.

In the field of health and safety there is a triangle (Figure 1.1) attributed to the work of Frank E. Bird Jr in 1969[1] representing the numbers of increasingly serious accidents in the construction industry in the United States, with the least serious along the base and the most serious at the peak. Bird examined 1,753,498 accidents and deduced from Heinrich's law[2] that the more accidents that happen, represented by the base of the triangle, then by proportion the more serious accidents will occur at the top of the triangle. Reduce the number in the base, and the number of serious accidents will reduce in proportion.

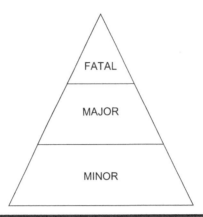

Figure 1.1 Bird's safety triangle.

The aim is then, obviously, to reduce the size of the base of the triangle, working towards what is described as 'zero defects'.

Patient safety is no different; the broader the base of minor incidents, then the more likely it will be that extremely serious incidents will occur.

James Reason, a professor at Manchester University, has proposed a model for such accidents (Figure 1.2).[3] He proposes that the controls to prevent errors are like slices of Swiss cheese, each slice having a number of small holes in it, each hole being a weakness in that control. So long as the holes in successive layers of cheese do not line up then no serious harm will be done. If, however, the hole in the next layer of control, the next slice of cheese, happens to be in line, then another layer of control will fail. If holes in every slice of cheese line up then all the controls will have failed, and a serious accident will occur.

This theory explains why serious accidents occur when a number of less serious errors occur together. Matthew Syed,[4] in his book

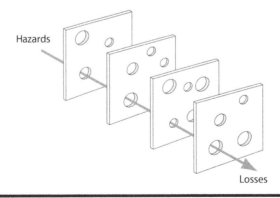

Figure 1.2 Reason's Swiss Cheese Model. (Illustration courtesy of Davidmack used under the Creative Commons Attribution Share Alike 3.0 unported license.)

Black Box Thinking: The Surprising Truth about Success (And Why Some People Never Learn from Their Mistakes), quotes the case of the unfortunate death of a 37-year-old mother who was admitted to hospital for a relatively straightforward sinus operation. For this patient, several things went wrong together.

After being anaesthetised, her jaw muscles tightened; the anaesthetist found that even the smallest laryngeal mask did not fit the patient; in response, the anaesthetist attempted a tracheal intubation but could not see the airway at the back of the throat; the nurses anticipated what should have happened next and prepared for a tracheostomy; although they informed the consultants, they were ignored; thinking that the consultants knew best they did not press further; the consultants continued to struggle to supply oxygen without a tracheostomy but lost track of time; by then the patient was starved of oxygen enough to become irreversibly injured, and she died some days later. Four unfortunate events all came together during the one operation, with fatal results. The holes in the slices of cheese all lined up.

Any of us could experience something similar at home. Imagine having to tell this story at home after the event.

'If only I had tidied up the boys' toys I would not have stepped on the roller skates; if only I had not been carrying a basket of washing I might have seen them; if only I had put the vacuum away I would not have tripped over the electric flex; if only I had put the chip pan on the back burner the handle would not have been sticking out; if only the baby had not been sitting by the stove she would not have been under the pan when it fell!' All the small mistakes came together at the same time; each of the five 'if onlys' was a slice of cheese, and all the holes lined up, allowing the accident to happen.

These illustrations show how the simplest errors can combine. As James Reason's model shows, the most serious incidents are usually when a combination of smaller faults all occur simultaneously. They also provide strong justification for a zero tolerance attitude to mistakes at work and, combined with a principle known as '1% better at 1000 things' (sometimes called 'marginal gains'), explained later in Chapter 4, help to overcome complacency towards minor issues. The heavy construction equipment company JCB has a (French) saying that sums up this idea *Jamais Content* – never be content.

Complacency is a dangerous attitude even when directed at only minor problems, simply because it spreads to more serious issues and if not corrected can affect everything, what might be called 'complacency creep'. In addition, who can draw the line that separates a minor problem from a serious problem? In a complex healthcare situation, who knows all of the knock-on effects of a small error?

Having recognised that 'A lesson could be learned', the process to do it is clear enough, as shown in Table 1.1, but its execution – making it happen – is less clear.

These are the questions addressed in this book.

Table 1.1 How Lessons Are Learned: The 11 Questions to Be Answered

We could do better here!

1. What happened?
2. Can we identify the causes that made it happen?
3. What do we have to do to eliminate the causes?
4. What new methods do we need?
5. What new equipment/software do we need?
6. Who do we have to retrain in the new processes?
7. Who do we have to tell about the new processes?
8. How do we tell them?
9. How do we check that this never happens again?
10. How can the whole organisation learn from this?
11. When should we audit the new processes, and who will carry out the audit?

Chapter 2

The Importance of Many Recent Reports

SUMMARY

The National Health Service (NHS) has made provision for about £50 billion for future negligence claims. Many of the opportunities for improvements to patient safety and for making associated financial savings are stated in some recent UK NHS reports, namely the Francis, Berwick and Kirkup reports; Professor Tim Briggs' 'Getting it Right First Time'; the Care Quality Commission (CQC) inspection reports; the NHS Safety Thermometer updates.

Negligence Claims: Improvements for the Sake of Costs Alone

In its Business Plan 2017/2018,[1] NHS Resolution, the not-for-profit organisation previously named the NHS Litigation Authority,[2] tasked with providing indemnity cover for legal claims against the NHS, made provision for £50.8 billion to meet all known and outstanding clinical claims for many years ahead, until each claim terminates. Using data from the NHS Confederation,[3] this is equivalent to £38,543 per employee (1.318 million) or 43% of running costs of £117 billion per annum. As part of this provision, NHS Resolution has budgeted £1.95 billion for projected medical negligence expenditure in the 12 months of 2017/18. This is 1.7% of the annual budget of about £117 billion, £1500 per employee per annum; enough to train 6500 new doctors, according to the Medical Protection Society (June 2017).[4]

Add to that the cost of the time and effort spent by the professionals concerned in defending themselves, and it is obviously a huge financial burden that would sink most private companies.

In addition, behind each claim will be a tragic family story of pain and suffering that no amount of financial compensation can alleviate.

Take another statistic. According to the Office of National Statistics (ONS), in 2009 there were 706,248 live births and 3688 stillbirths.[5] Infant deaths (deaths before the age of 12 months) added another 3500 deaths, making a total of over 7000 families devastated by the loss of a child under 12 months old, each year.

In the United States, Michelle M. Mello et al., in their 2009 paper 'National Costs of the Medical Liability System',[6] have estimated that overall annual medical liability system costs are estimated to be $55.6 billion in '2008' dollars, 2.4% of total annual healthcare spending.

Thirty years ago, during the push for better quality across industry started by British Prime Minister Margaret Thatcher, these costs would have been labelled 'The cost of poor quality' and would have been the target for a major improvement programme in any progressive business. The NHS now has such programmes running.

The Francis, Berwick and Kirkup Reports: Improvements in Patient Safety

Much of the evidence for justifying this book is presented in three government reports.

In February 2013 Sir Robert Francis presented a report into the failings at the Mid Staffordshire NHS Foundation Trust[7] during the period 2005 to 2009 when between 400 and 1200 patients died as a result of poor care.

Then in August 2013 the National Advisory Group on the Safety of Patients in England under the guidance of Dr. Don Berwick produced 'Improving the Safety of Patients in England', commonly known as the Berwick Report,[8] addressing the findings of the Francis Report.

Dr. Berwick made 10 recommendations to resolve the problems highlighted by the Francis Report. Four in particular are relevant to this book:

Berwick Recommendation 1

The NHS should continually and forever reduce patient harm by embracing wholeheartedly an ethic of learning.

Berwick Recommendation 5

Mastery of quality and patient safety sciences and practices should be part of initial preparation and lifelong education of all health care professionals, including managers and executives.

Berwick Recommendation 6

The NHS should become a learning organisation. Its leaders should create and support the capability for learning, and therefore change, at scale, within the NHS.

Berwick Recommendation 7

Transparency should be complete, timely and unequivocal. All data on quality and safety, whether assembled by government, organisations, or professional societies, should be shared in a timely fashion with all parties who want it, including, in accessible form, with the public.

Additional Berwick Comments

In addition, the Berwick Report said that the system in the NHS in England must

- *'Abandon blame as a tool and trust the goodwill and good intentions of the staff'.*
- *'Recognise that transparency is essential and expect and insist on it'.*
- *'Ensure that responsibility for functions related to safety and improvement are vested clearly and simply'.*

- *'Give the people of the NHS career-long help to learn, master and apply modern methods for quality control, quality improvement and quality planning'.*
- *'Make sure pride and joy in work, not fear, infuse the NHS'.*

All of these principles are based on the following understanding of quality and patient safety stated on page 11 of the Berwick Report.

> *Whereas some modern industries define 'quality' as the degree to which a system of production meets or exceeds the needs and desires of the people it serves, Lord Darzi in his reports in 2007 and 2008 defined quality for the NHS as comprising three dimensions Safety (avoiding harm from the care that is intended to help) Effectiveness (aligning care with science and ensuring efficiency) Patient-experience (including patient-centeredness, timeliness and equity).*
> *An effective quality management system includes quality control (to keep sound processes reliable on a daily basis), quality improvement (to decrease variation within and among NHS organisations so that the best becomes the norm) and quality planning (especially fostering innovative care models that can deliver better outcomes at lower cost).*

The Kirkup Report

In March 2015, 'The Report of the Morecambe Bay Investigation' by Dr. Bill Kirkup was published.[9] This investigation was established by the Secretary of State for Health to examine concerns raised over the deaths of mothers and babies between 1 January 2004 and 30 June 2013 at what became the University Hospitals of Morecambe Bay NHS Foundation Trust.

In paragraph 5 of the executive summary, the report states that

> *it found 20 instances of significant or major failures of care at Furness General Hospital associated with three maternal deaths and the deaths of 16 babies at or shortly after birth.*

This was almost four times the frequency of such failures at the Royal Lancaster Infirmary.

In paragraph 6 of the Executive Summary, the report states

> *These problems did not occur overnight ... . It is however vital that incidents are properly investigated in order to identify problems and prevent a recurrence.*

The report goes on to identify failings at all levels of management to identify the basic causes of the unacceptable deaths. Finally, in Chapter 8 of the report, 'Conclusions and Recommendations', there are 44 recommendations mostly addressing how, at all levels of management, there should be serious changes to attitudes, skills and ways of working. But recommendation 12, in particular, states,

> *The University Hospitals of Morecambe Bay NHS Foundation Trust should review the structures, processes and staff involved in investigating incidents, carrying out root cause analyses, reporting results and disseminating learning from incidents,*

and there is the inference from paragraph 6 of the Executive Summary that these root causes should be removed to prevent recurrence.

This book explains how root cause analysis is done. It takes methods used over the last 40 years in business and industry which are applicable to the work of people who deal with patients in the health service and allows the reader to connect these methods to the recommendations of the Berwick Report.

Stillbirth Statistics

The charity Sands[10] has highlighted maternity statistics from the ONS[11] that in England and Wales in 2014 there were 3254 stillbirths and 695,233 live births, equating to 4.7 per 1000 births; this is 9 per day.

According to *The Lancet*[12] (using different data), the United Kingdom is joint 21st worst in the world for stillbirths − 20 other countries are better. This is a very worrying level for a leading economic country in Western Europe.

As there are about 155 maternity units in the United Kingdom, there will be on average 21 stillbirths every year per unit or one every 17 days in each unit. There is now a national collaborative reporting project Mothers and Babies: Reducing Risk through Audits and Confidential Enquiries across the United Kingdom (MBRRACE-UK)[13] reporting results nationally so that improvement action can be taken.

This is the national-level picture for which the Morecambe Bay Trust is a specific, local example where a number of personal tragedies became a national statistic.

Sands[9] the charity lists more than eight possible causes of baby deaths but goes further and adds that around one-half of these baby deaths are 'unexplained' – there was no clear cause. This topic alone would lend itself to the methods described in this book, namely the problem-solving process, process mapping, cause and effect analysis, run charting, solution effect analysis and coordinated retraining.

Each of the eight known causes would be the subject of its own cause and effect analysis, and statistical evidence would direct researchers to the most common causes that would take priority for elimination.

This technique is called 'drilling down', going into finer and finer detail until investigators can go no further.

Getting It Right First Time: Professor Briggs

In September 2012, Professor Timothy Briggs presented a report to the British Orthopaedic Association, 'Getting it Right First Time'.[14] In this report, Professor Briggs states that by finding the best practice in orthopaedic surgery and copying it across the NHS, significant improvements can be made in patient satisfaction, reduced litigation costs, reduced running costs and reduced waiting times. This approach is called benchmarking best practice, a technique in which the methods used by the best operators of a method or system, anywhere in the world, are copied. The classic example of this is the refuelling and wheel changing of Formula One race cars, the system copied from Formula One being the use of critical path analysis to speed up a process.

Care Quality Commission Report on Hospitals

In October 2015, the CQC in 'The state of health care and adult social care in England 2014/15' published the results of revised inspections across health and social care.[1] The report summary picks out the following points relevant to this book:

> *There is a (large) variation in the quality of care between different services and different providers.*
> *In inspections to the end of May 2015, 7% of the services were rated inadequate, the care is so poor urgent improvements are needed.*
> *One in ten hospitals were rated inadequate, as was 10% of social care services and 6% of primary medical services.*
> *A range of factors affect the safety of services, including a failure to investigate incidents properly and learn from them so they do not happen again (i.e. eliminate the root causes).*
> *It is vital to have feedback mechanisms to know whether or not changes have been successful.*
> *Every provider should have good benchmarked data for all the services it provides to assure itself that it is providing safe and effective care and to know where improvements are needed.*

With this latest report a very clear picture of the action required is emerging, but what is less clear is 'How to do it'. This book sets out to explain many of these points.

The NHS Safety Thermometer

In 2010 the Quality, Innovation, Productivity and Prevention (QIPP) safe care national programme[16] sought to improve the quality of patient safety. In January 2016, a report[17] was published by the Health & Social Care Information Centre giving the results of the national survey into four harms – pressure ulcers, falls with harm, urinary tract infections and new venous thromboembolisms. The report with three tables and six charts illustrates the data from December 2014 to December 2015. In the author's view this is a major step forward in the collection and analysis of key data for improving patient safety in 'care delivery settings' and sets an excellent pattern for examining other common problems.

A summary of the reported results showed that for a 13-month period, 2.66 million patients in up to 861 organisations, between 93.8% and 94.3% of patients were 'harm free' (Tables 2 and 3 of the report). At first sight 93.8%

harm free appears to be good, but reversing the emphasis and expressing the result as 'not harm free' means between 5.7% and 6.2% (1 in every 17 patients or about 152,000) suffered harm by one of the four categories of harm.

There is obviously much more detailed work needed to reduce these numbers.

(All data quoted from the QIPP report, copyright © 2016, used with the permission of the Health and Social Care Information Centre. All rights reserved.)

Chapter 3

Primary and Secondary Care in the NHS and Long-Term Care

SUMMARY

Opportunities for improvement can be classified into different types that need different problem-solving approaches. Large problems should be broken down into smaller ones. Some can be resolved locally, others need national support.

The National Health Service and Long-Term Care

Since 1948 a unique healthcare system has been created in Britain. The National Health Service (NHS) has many points of contact with its patients from the primary care of general practitioners (GPs), dentists, physiotherapists, psychiatrists and community nursing through the secondary care of hospitals. Then there is a separate system of longer-term care in nursing and care homes.

There are four independently managed NHS organisations in England, Scotland, Wales and Northern Ireland. In addition, when anyone is fit enough not to need hospital treatment but incapable of living at home they will need nursing and residential care that is not part of the NHS but run by local councils and funded separately.

Any patient can pass through any combination of these providers, with each provider trying to give the best service over their specific field of expertise.

The four NHS organisations have no competition; no other organisations provide any UK citizen with healthcare 'free at the point of delivery' and 'from cradle to grave'. They are 'not-for-profit' organisations and deal with very complex problems – sick people. Often the outcome is not what was hoped for, not because of mistakes but because of the complexity of the human body.

Why is the lack of competition important? In the case of the world-class units in the NHS it is less important, but in the case of those units that have officially been found to be wanting it is very important. Local public opinion probably knew long before the authorities did that there were problems, and had there been a local alternative the services of the alternative would have been used. People would have 'voted with their feet', something that they cannot do with the NHS.

At the time of finishing this book in May 2017, over a bank holiday weekend, British Airways' information technology (IT) systems failed completely worldwide, and thousands of air travellers were left stranded at airports all over the world. Many of these people when they travel by air in future will have a choice of airline; they can vote with their feet. Obviously, British Airways did not apply the same failure elimination criteria to its IT systems that it does to flight safety!

Now that healthcare advances and scientific discoveries have ways to ameliorate and cure many of the diseases that once were so devastating such as smallpox, diphtheria, cholera, tuberculosis and typhoid, the healthcare services across the advanced world are left with the more complex problems, the more serious illnesses, like pancreatic cancer, that are more difficult to cure and dementia, that is difficult to prevent and treat.

People are living longer and now have higher expectations for their health than in 1948 when the NHS was founded. The medication used is very expensive to develop and costs more to treat the patients. Equipment is getting more complex and expensive.

Dividing the Elephant into Bite-Size Chunks

There are many different types of problems facing healthcare, for example waiting times and 'never events' (defined officially as incidents that should never happen), and a vast improvement programme is being driven by

Health England.[1] Each of the following different types of problem requires its own approach to make improvements.

Indeed, when making improvements within an organisation it is important to analyse the problems carefully and break each down into its simplest elements, to provide a coherent and logical plan, otherwise a chaotic shambles will result, like the little boys' football team where everyone chases the ball at the same time.

In the following paragraphs I have divided what I perceive to be the major problem areas in the British health service into seven different problem types, popularly called eating the elephant by dividing it into bite-sized chunks.

Type 1 Timescales, Waiting Lists, Waiting Times, Capacity and Capability (See Chapter 9)

It is logical that any service unit, a GP or dental practice, community care, long-term care or a hospital, will be able to cope with a certain level of demand, known as capacity, determined at some planning stage. Should that demand level be exceeded then the system will be overloaded and become technically 'incapable' of delivering the required standard until the required level of capacity is increased.

Most businesses have periods of high demand, sometimes predictable like Christmas and other religious festivals, sometimes not. Often they cope by having only enough permanent employees to cover the lower levels of business and using temporary workers at seasonal times of overload. In this way they do not have workers idle during periods of low demand.

The NHS faces both that phenomenon and the problem of constantly increasing demand as the population expects higher levels of healthcare. Higher demand is good news for a profit-making organisation but bad news for a free service one, financed by taxes.

Waiting times in hospitals are governed by (1) the incidence of major accidents, terrorist activity and seasonal epidemics, some of which occur at random and cannot be anticipated, interfering with the elective work which has been planned; and (2) the availability of both adequate funding and trained people to provide the resources to meet the demands of a modern health-conscious population.

Unfortunately, there always seems to be a shortage of funding, so resources are never enough and the planners have to 'do their best', juggling between elective and emergency work. However, through innovation, efficiencies can be increased using better methods of working.

Type 2 Never Events (See Chapter 13)

The term 'never events' has a specific meaning within the NHS, and instances are defined on the NHS England website.[1] Twelve are defined for Surgical and Medication such as wrong site surgery, wrong implant prosthesis and retained foreign objects. Another 2 are defined for Mental Health, 10 more for General Healthcare and 1 for Maternity, making a total of 25.

A challenging feature of never events is that they occur very infrequently at single locations but are not uncommon over the NHS as a whole.

The data for never events is being collated in 2016 by the Patient Safety Domain Team of NHS England, and a press release has been issued (February 2016) by the Patients Association showing that there have been about 1100 such events in the past 4 years.[2] With 1760 hospitals alone, the statistics show that there is only one never event every 5 years per hospital. Using another statistic from the NHS Confederation,[3] there are about 10 million procedures a year in the NHS so the probability of a never event happening is 30 for every million procedures. These are very broad-based statistics and not meant to be definitive or a yardstick, only to show a general pattern.

The fact that they occur so infrequently at a given location means that in that unit they could be seen as one-offs and not taken as seriously as they should be. It is possible because of this infrequency that the employees at that unit have never dealt with a never event and would not know how to handle one. In turn, because blame is a strong element in any investigation into this type of problem, and because the occurrence is infrequent, there will be a desire to be defensive and cover up the event. (Over 50 years in business, I have seen much of this).

These factors would justify the NHS setting up 'never events' flying squads that would investigate each one independently. At 250 incidents a year, five a week, it would be kept quite busy. However, every workplace where a never event occurs must take full responsibility for it immediately, find the cause and eliminate the cause as soon as possible, which is the standard quality assurance approach.

The number of these 'never events' can be reduced by using methods such as 'cause and effect analysis' and 'process flowcharting', and then monitored with 'statistical trend analysis' as the NHS is now doing.

In an organisation such as the health service, there is no need for a fragmented approach to problem solving where each surgical team solves its own problems, wasting time through the duplication of methods. Through the sharing of information between health trusts, acceptable zero defect methods can be agreed and communicated to each other given the right incentives.

However, people will be more willing to accept imposed change if they understand why the new methods are being recommended to them, otherwise the 'Not invented here' syndrome will kick in.

Type 3 Unacceptable Trends (See Chapter 15)

Sudden outbreaks of infection, poor quality surgery, mortality rates, stillbirths, poor quality of care and similar all need to be detected and recognized at source in the first place. This is achieved by statistically monitoring the numbers occurring using basic quality control methods. A statistically significant increase in undesirable results should kick start an investigation of possible causes, and the implementation of improved methods should produce a reduction of the number of occurrences to, hopefully, zero. For these methods to work the numbers recorded must be accurate, and the people using them must be scrupulously honest. Sweeping the facts under the carpet only makes the situation worse.

The NHS Safety Thermometer[4] referred to in Chapter 2 has now been introduced to help make improvements in this type of problem

Type 4 Wasteful Quick Fixes (See Solution Effect Analysis, Chapter 20)

This type of problem is any action taken to discharge a patient that results in the return of the patient and impacts on Type 1 problems of queuing and reducing throughput. It is a short-term gain with a longer-term cost, and, more importantly, it endangers the patient.

Every time a patient returns the reasons for return must be recorded and, with cause and effect analysis, rules for safer discharge imposed, together with appropriate training.

Type 5 How to Function More Smoothly (See Chapter 9)

All workplaces have their own idiosyncrasies, and local teams can usually find better ways of working. Unfortunately, the need to make changes is not always obvious and apparent; someone is needed who can spot opportunities and convince their fellow team members to do something about it. This handbook describes the techniques that can be used in these circumstances.

Type 6 Leadership Style, Attitude and Ability, the Culture

The BBC reported in 2012 that the NHS, with 1,700,000 employees, is the fifth largest employer in the world after the US Department of Defense, the Peoples' Liberation Army of China, Walmart and McDonalds.[4] The figure 1.7 million must be regarded as an approximate number because staffing levels are constantly changing.

To provide first-class care, every single person should be fully trained, reliable, motivated, a team player, caring and compassionate. It would be hard to estimate what percentage of 1.7 million people will meet all 6 criteria.

The Francis, Berwick and Kirkup reports, described earlier, list the shortcomings in attitude and behaviour found in the two hospital trusts investigated, and only action taken at the very highest management and political level will ensure that improvements will be made. It will require strong, courageous leadership at all levels to create a culture of constant improvement in every corner of the health service.

Type 7 Bullying and Harassment

There are four different ways that bullying and harassment can be interpreted: patients bullying patients, patients bullying those treating them, healthcare professionals bullying patients and healthcare professionals bullying each other.

Obviously all of these are unacceptable, and in an organisation of 1.7 million there will be many instances of the four types. Unfortunately, when it is discovered it hits the headlines in the media, and the whole organisation becomes tarnished.

It is not easy to discover this problem, for various reasons. Patients might think it is just the professional's bedside manner and put up with it to allow their treatment to be completed. Staff might have difficulty bringing the matter to the attention of someone independent and might fear retribution such as victimisation or the loss of their job.

Regardless of these fears, bullying and harassment of any form is counter-productive and is an opportunity for improvement just as much as bed sores and falls.

Overview

Each of the seven problem types just listed requires a different methodology for recording, communicating, analysing and resolving the detail, and these methods are described later in the book.

To summarise, the causes of many of the problems in the NHS and long-term care are lack of funds, misuse of funds, overworked units, lack of care, poor communications, poor record keeping, inadequate training and, above all, poor leadership and supervision. This book is more about resolving practical problems than changing attitudes and behaviour, but by getting as many people as possible to work on successful improvement projects it will help do just that.

How Will People Know When to Take Action?

All the time, every work team leader should be asking 'how can we improve by

- Doing fewer (bad things) and more (good things)
- Getting faster results
- Spending less time on wasteful activities?'

then, with the team, following the methods described later in Chapter 11 onwards.

Progress and Success

Mo Mowlem was Secretary of State for Northern Ireland, and in the work leading up to the Good Friday agreement in 1998 used the phrase in a television interview 'The status quo is not acceptable' to justify the need for change. The Francis, Berwick and Kirkup reports all imply that the current status quo is not acceptable.

So what defines and makes a world-beating health care service? I suggest

- A clear purpose focusing on patient safety and comfort
- Proven values, methods and rules shared by all
- Trained people at every level
- First-class resources
- Strong leadership
- A commitment to continuously improve everywhere.

Many people would say that the British NHS is world beating, and perhaps in many parts it is, but do the aforementioned qualities apply to 100% or 80% or 50% or x%? The reports on the Mid Staffordshire NHS Foundation Trust and the University Hospitals Morecambe Bay NHS Foundation Trust would suggest there is still room for much improvement.

Chapter 4

1% Better at 1000 Things

SUMMARY

'If you always do what you have always done you will always get what you have always got'.

Henry Ford

Small incremental or marginal improvements are just as important as the major ones. They reduce the base of the Bird's triangle. Complacency creep is challenged.

Having been a quality assurance and business excellence specialist I have taken a touchline view of the National Health Service (NHS) for many years. In that time, I have seen many examples where I have felt a continuous improvement attitude to work would have been beneficial. In the 1980s, Jan Carlzon helped turn around Scandinavian Air Services using the catchphrase 'you can't change something by 1000 times but you can change 1000s of things by 1%'.[1] The current philosophy of making 'marginal gains' is the modern equivalent of this 1980s concept.

   Every day we might see practical examples where there is an opportunity to do better by a small amount, but many people will not recognise the opportunity or the need to change. With good leadership they can be shown why and how it can be done. The following examples are just a small sample of the opportunities out there waiting for someone to make some changes for the better.

As I explained in Chapter 1, the more inefficiencies and minor errors there are at the base of the Bird's triangle, the greater chance there is of a major error occurring. Then the more major errors there are, the greater the chance there is of a more serious error occurring.

Now that the Francis, Berwick and Kirkup reports are providing the high-level guidelines for a total change of working in the health service, it is appropriate to describe how their thinking could apply at ground level.

Here are some personally acquired examples to explain what I mean.

'Nil by Mouth'

I have always believed that the Nil by Mouth rule was very important. A patient before an operation under anaesthetic must not have food in their stomach. Nor should food be given after certain operations until the digestive system has recovered and is ready for food (RCN Guidelines: Perioperative Fasting in Adults and Children; November 2005[2]). I knew of a patient whose recovery was severely compromised, needing a second invasive operation when they were given food after an operation because that important message 'had not got through'. Indeed, 5 years on that patient has had further complications requiring much more invasive surgery as a knock-on effect of the initial error.

Again, in 2014 another patient had appendicitis and was waiting to go to theatre. This was delayed because of some urgent trauma cases. During the 6-hour wait several anaesthetists saw the patient, and then on three separate occasions over a couple of hours, different assistants offered the patient a drink from the trolley. The patient, being of sound mind, declined, but on the third attempt the patient's visitor looked to see how 'Nil by Mouth' was displayed to prevent food or drink being given. What they found was a scrap of torn-off paper with N B M hand-scribbled on it in pencil!

When challenged about a more professional method of signalling the message, the ward sister explained that smarter, printed, laminated notices were in the desk drawer but had been banned by the Infection Control Department. There was no effective means for signalling 'Nil by Mouth', and amazingly no one challenged that ruling.

One can understand the politics of the situation – infection cases at that time were being counted, monitored and reported at a high management level, whereas problems caused by patients having food during an operation are probably less high profile politically.

There has always been a need for Nil by Mouth signs in hospital wards, certainly all my lifetime. Why, in such a large professional organisation as the NHS, has an approved acceptable method not been agreed and made standard practice? Or, if it has, why was it ignored at that hospital?

Would anyone know how many times in a month, across all the hospitals in England, do patients have to have corrective treatment because the Nil by Mouth care was compromised?

If all these failures of the system were monitored and costed there would be enough evidence to drive through a standard method of working.

Be 1% better at 1000 things.

'The Urine Sample': An Example of a Small Continuous Improvement

Not all opportunities for improvement have far-reaching consequences, but they can be time-wasting and irritating, indicating a lack of care and attention to detail.

In this true incident, a patient was due to have a pre-assessment for an invasive operation and was asked to bring an early morning urine sample to the hospital assessment clinic two days before the operation, but a sample bottle was not provided. So what would the average person use for the sample? In this case a jam jar, with a screw-top lid, both suitably washed, dried and put in a plastic bag.

The patient was seen by the nurse who told the patient that the urine sample was unusable because of the possibility of trace amounts of sugar from the original contents contaminating it, even though everything had been washed.

The nurse took the jar and its contents for disposal. No urine test was done, but the nurse gave the patient a new sample bottle with a screw cap to bring a sample on the day of the operation.

Two observations arise from this event. First, if jam jars are not acceptable, why was this not pointed out in the patient's letter and a suitable alternative recommended; or better still, why was a sample bottle not provided in the first place?

The second point is that if it was acceptable to wait until the day of the operation to provide a sample of urine, was the earlier sample really needed? If the advance nature of the testing had been really essential, then several days would have been lost and delays incurred. So what was the better option?

Many people would think that this is a very minor point, but considering that urine testing has been taking place since the ancient Egyptians tested for diabetes in 1550 Bc (3500 years ago), the process for getting the results without a hitch, even in 2014, is still subject to simple errors. It wasted both the nurse's and the patient's time and puzzled and annoyed the patient!

That nurse would think nothing of the incident, but suppose that one in five patients made the same error, in every hospital, every day, for several years, how much time could be saved?

But then there is another unseen benefit to highlighting this incident. Discussing it starts to get all those involved in thinking about the principal of not tolerating silly, irritating methods and discovering that with some careful thought, small improvements can be made all the time.

Be 1% better at 1000 things.

Phone Calls Not Made

I know of many cases, involving personal acquaintances, where during a phone call for an appointment or test results the patient was told by the health worker: 'I will telephone you back this afternoon'. After waiting in the house all afternoon and the call does not come, the patient has a dilemma: 'Shall I or shall I not call back?' Perhaps they need to go out, say to get medication for the person they are caring for. Strictly, this is unacceptable service, but many people make excuses saying that the person they are dealing with is busy, and they do not want to disturb them. So time is wasted because of poor work discipline – a promise is a promise, anything else is unprofessional.

Be 1% better at 1000 things.

Errors of Communication

A patient was in hospital for an operation. Afterwards in recovery he had a minor heart attack. The following day a nurse told him she was to give him two injections that morning. He questioned the reason for this, and the nurse said she would check. She returned and told the patient that the injections were not necessary. What would have been the result if he had not challenged the nurse? It took a sick patient to provide his own quality control. What if he had not had the presence of mind or the courage to do this?

Be 1% better at 1000 things.

Letters to Patients

The patient was due to have a computed tomography (CT) colonography examination, a three-dimensional x-ray of the abdomen. The patient was sent a letter and a bottle of Gastrografin, which would have arrived at his home on the Saturday before the scan. However, the postman could not put the package through the letterbox, and the patient was not in the house. Consequently, the package had to be picked up from the sorting office on Monday (irritation #1). The letter announced that the scan would be on Thursday, would the patient have a blood sample taken two days before the scan, that is Tuesday (a bit tight to organise, irritation #2) and follow the fasting instructions on the Wednesday. There was also a diet sheet for the fasting day, outlining a strict set of instructions to ensure that the examination would be effective. These instructions stated that the patient should continue to take all medicines that they normally took except two specific ones, neither of which the patient was taking. However, the patient was normally taking Fybogel, a bulking agent, and he guessed it might be a problem. The letter gave a telephone number to ring with queries, so on the Monday he rang the number to ask about Fybogel. That was when a further complication arose: a voicemail was in operation asking the caller to leave any message, but this was a question that needed an answer quickly (irritation #3)! He left his number for a call back, but that didn't happen, this was like a dead end because call backs cannot be relied upon (irritation #4). Luckily the blood sample was to be taken at the same hospital a day before the procedure, and the patient was able to visit the radiology department that sent the letter out. When he asked whether he should or should not take the Fybogel, he was told definitely not. So why did the letter not say so (final irritation #5)? It all worked out satisfactorily in the end, but not without a lot of hassle. The expression 'Joined-up writing' springs to mind.

Be 1% better at 1000 things.

Day-to-Day Errors

A patient was recovering four days after a serious bowel operation. Early in the morning the nurse removed the catheter. When the registrar came on his rounds he was surprised it had been removed without his authority because he considered that it should have remained in place for longer. He ordered that it should be replaced. Two nurses unsuccessfully attempted to refit it and needed a third person to finally put it in place. It was a very distressing and annoying experience for the patient, especially as they had a full bladder at the time. It was not removed for a further four days.

Because of an error of judgement an unnecessary ultrasound scan had to be carried out, and two nurses and two doctors spent about 30 minutes making the patient comfortable. Two man hours of time that could have been spent on more productive work were wasted. This is called 'The Cost of Poor Quality'. It was unlikely that anyone pointed the error out to the nurse who removed the catheter. An opportunity for improvement was missed.

Be 1% better at 1000 things.

Mislaid Results

I am reminded of a very ill friend who was being treated by two hospitals. On several occasions, he had problems when his test results were lost in transmission between the different units. By the time they were found it was too late for them to be used effectively, and repeats had to be made and used. I wonder whether the participants in this process realised they were steps in a process and whether, when that process broke down, they realised that there was a quality problem. Perhaps it was the first time this had happened to the people concerned and they thought nothing of it, but if a survey had been carried out in the whole organisation, would it have revealed that documents were being lost each week? There was an opportunity here for a continuous improvement project.

If situations like that happen frequently they become the norm, and some people shrug their shoulders and move on. It would take a bold person to say 'Something is going wrong here, can we do something to stop it happening again?', and at the same time they don't want to get their work colleagues 'into trouble'.

Be 1% better at 1000 things.

Don't 'Shoot Yourself in the Foot'

The problems facing the NHS are difficult enough without people 'shooting themselves in the foot'. The time saved by reducing 'unforced errors' (as they say in tennis) could then be spent on the serious, difficult and challenging work.

Finding the Time to Make Improvements

Often when people are challenged about why improvements are not made the answer is that they do not have the time, but as the previous examples show, they have to make time to do the job twice!

Chapter 5

Be Inspired: Innovation throughout History

SUMMARY

It has been man's ability to innovate that has given us the amazing technological advances that we have today. The ability to write our thoughts down to record and pass on information and agree what we mean has been one of the most critical 'inventions'. It is essential that we continue to invent and so create a safer, healthier world.

Continuous Improvement and Innovation

Making improvements is not only about learning from mistakes, it is also about innovation, trying new ideas and developing them until they can be shown to produce significant benefits. Once that has been demonstrated they can be cascaded across the whole of the organisation; organ transplants, artificial joints, stem cells and gene therapy are good examples, as is creating body parts by three-dimensional computer aided printing.

There have been many breakthrough discoveries and inventions over the last 3000 years – writing, the printing press, the electron microscope and transistors, to name a few. Each invention has then been improved incrementally until we have the refinements we know today. The refinements have been like the 1% at 1000 things mentioned earlier.

Homo sapiens, the Inventor

For over 200,000 years *Homo sapiens* (the human race) has used ingenuity and passion to change our way of life to the point where we can hardly imagine what could be improved further. Fire has become the modern kitchen oven and the industrial furnace, the wheel has become the car, a magnifying glass has become the electron microscope and the Romans' heliograph has become the Internet.

Modern materials allow us to make fabrics, devices and buildings much stronger and lighter, which, combined with our knowledge of the sciences, has led to spacesuits, semiconductors and supersonic aircraft.

Modern medicine and the biological sciences have produced antibiotics, artificial hearts, stem cells and gene therapy.

Professor Brian Cox, in his BBC TV episode 'From Caveman to Spaceman',[1] has recently described how he believes that being able to write and read has been the biggest influence on human progress. Only by writing down what we are thinking can someone else understand our thoughts and then challenge them with their own ideas. This is just as important in the 21st century as it was 5000 years ago when the Egyptians built the Pyramids, and is fundamental to continuous improvement. Unless we express our thoughts clearly in a way other people understand, and document them so that the point cannot be forgotten or distorted, we will only cause confusion. Even when one participant writes down their version of the agreement, the other participant can interpret differently from the other. Several written versions may be needed before there is agreement. Our listener will think they understand what we are thinking, but without documenting it, how will we all know exactly what is being said? (I am discounting political situations where confusion is deliberate so that meaning can be spun after the event.)

Verbal communication can be confusing. The speaker knows what he/she meant (or thinks he/she does). The listener thinks he knows what he heard. Joint agreement can be a fraction of the total. Two Venn diagrams help to explain this.

In Figure 5.1, the left-hand circle represents what the speaker thought they had asked for. The right-hand circle represents the listener's opinion of what they thought they heard. Where the circles overlap, shown by cross hatching, represents agreement. The listener provided what the speaker wanted.

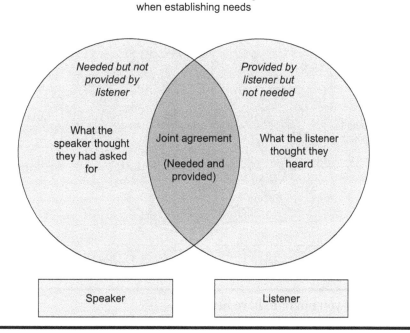

Figure 5.1 What you thought you heard.

Obviously, in the ideal situation the two circles would overlap completely. This is represented by Figure 5.2, representing perfect harmony, just what any healthcare worker should be aiming for.

The ideal situation is when the two circles coincide completely. This fact-finding process can be carried out through first, reflective listening in which the listener constantly plays back what they understand to the speaker, using the listener's terminology. When this happens the speaker will often say 'Oh no, I didn't mean that!' At the end the listener should write down what he has learned and allow the speaker to agree, and even sign the notes.

This is also very important for what can be called 'corporate intelligence', which for this purpose is the sum total of the knowledge of the organisation. When knowledge of the technical specialisms of a business, that is healthcare, is written down, it is accessible to all. When it is only in the memories of the participants then it is volatile and can leave the organisation if the individual leaves. Hence, the need to record everything that the employees learn as collective knowledge is very important.

People sometimes dispute to whom this knowledge (or intellectual property) belongs, but this is how 'lessons are learned'.

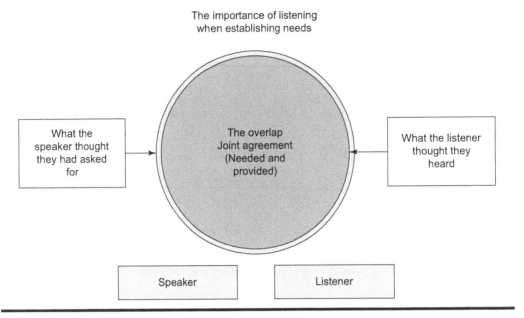

The importance of listening
when establishing needs

| What the speaker thought they had asked for | → | The overlap Joint agreement (Needed and provided) | ← | What the listener thought they heard |

Speaker   Listener

Figure 5.2   What you ought to have heard.

Some of the Significant Inventors

Continuing the story of innovation, Pythagoras, Archimedes and Euclid established some of the early principles of science.

The Magna Carta was the written agreement between King John and the English people in 1215.

Gutenberg developed the first printing press in 1440.

Dr. Johnson published a dictionary of the English language in 1755.

The US Constitution was signed in 1787.

Charles Darwin wrote *On the Origin of Species* in 1859.

Newton, Faraday, Brunel, Armstrong, Charles Rolls, Henry Royce and Marconi achieved outstanding progress in their particular fields of engineering and science.

More recently, Tim Berners-Lee, Steve Jobs, Mark Zuckerberg and Bill Gates have taken us into the digital age.

My prize for innovation in modern times goes to the inventor of the wind-up radio, Trevor Baylis. He took several existing technologies – radio, power storage (batteries) and electronics – and combined all the latest capabilities to create a hand-wound rechargeable radio that can be used anywhere there is a radio signal.

I hope that every reader will have their own favourite inventor.

In one area we have been less successful in making improvements, and that is in people management and the functioning of organisations. We now have psychologists, procedures, Twitter and emails, but are we any better now than the Egyptians, Greeks or Romans were 2000 years ago?

If we want to improve the society we live in and the organisations in which we work, it is necessary to apply similar disciplines for making management, organisational, social and interpersonal improvements to those that have been used to improve our technical and scientific abilities during the last 500 years.

There have been many ground-breaking inventions in my lifetime which I would like to share with the reader.

When my grandmother was born in 1891, the only rapid long-distance communication system was the electric telegraph using Morse code. It was the Internet of the day. By the time I was born radio was established, television was in its infancy and electronics still used electronic valves; antibiotics had not been made available commercially. Here are some personal anecdotes to illustrate the progress that has been made since then.

My GPS Route Tracker and the Inventions That Make It Work

I have many interests, of which mountain walking, maps and statistical measurements are a few. Until a couple of years ago I used Ordnance Survey (OS) maps and a compass when fell walking. If I wanted to plan a route I used a piece of string or a map measure to work out the distance, and I counted the contour lines to assess the height to be gained and descended. To make a height profile of the planned walk (a plot of height above sea level versus distance walked along the route) was very tedious and almost never created unless the walk needed careful time planning.

During the walk, progress was assessed against the landmarks and the physical features that were visible along the way. Afterwards, a few calculations would tell me the average speed, and perhaps the details would go into a diary.

Now in 2017 on a smartphone, I can view the map, the distance walked, the height gained or lost and other data that can be calculated from those measurements and stored for future reference in the (Internet) cloud. All of this technology is now taken for granted by millions of walkers, runners, cyclists and yachtsmen using their own specific devices and software.

Since those earlier days there has been so much technical innovation that the whole process of undertaking a moorland walk with the latest gizmos can, if you are not careful, become an extreme technological distraction, especially when global positioning system (GPS) contact is lost in a forest or the phone battery goes flat!

All of these advances have been made because people have sought to make improvements to the existing technology and have learned from their mistakes.

What Improvements Created the GPS App?

OS maps have become digitised. Instead of existing in two-dimensional form on a piece of paper, all the ground features have been converted into a computer code that allows them to be presented on a computer screen. This includes the height of the ground above sea level so that three-dimensional models of the terrain can be created and bird's-eye view fly-throughs generated as if the viewer was an eagle flying above it all.

The basic map data for the OS maps was first surveyed in the mid to late nineteenth century, and the first complete set of official maps of Great Britain was published in the 1890s. Imagine the work that went into surveying every square mile of Britain on foot, recording, checking and printing it, without computers to help! Now we have Google Earth and Street View.

Consider also the types of instruments available and the difficulties of standardising the measurements of distance and height.

One of the first steps in producing the maps was to establish a base line. In 1784 this base line, 5 miles long (nominally 26,400 feet) on Hounslow Heath in southwest London (now under Heathrow Airport) was set up to start a survey between London and Paris. The base line, against which all other measurements would be made, was measured with a calibrated 100-foot-long steel chain and lately, modern measuring techniques have shown that William Roy's measurement of 27,404.7 feet is now considered to be 27,376.8 feet, a difference over 5 miles of 27.9 feet!

The people involved in producing these maps from start to finish needed physical toughness, as in climbing over Scottish mountains and islands with theodolites; mathematical ingenuity for triangulating everything back to the base line; and meticulous record keeping to provide the data needed for dozens of map makers in the head office. The directors of these projects needed mental toughness and political skills both to drive the work and also to convince the establishment to support it and then back it financially.

Personal Computers

To be able to view a digital map out of doors on the hills one needs a compact, mobile, personal computing device.

The first commercial computer was an IBM SSEC, which in 1948 contained 12,500 vacuum tubes (radio valves) and could make thousands of calculations in seconds. It did not have a screen but produced results on punched paper tapes. By 1958 the valves had been replaced by transistors. In 1964, the IBM System 360 had a memory of up to 524,000 characters.

Calculating became faster, output used cathode ray tubes, data storage memories got larger and more compact, data input methods became easier and finally, Apple and Microsoft produced the first user-friendly interfaces in 1984/85. This was the birth of the personal computer or PC that so many of us are now familiar with.

Laptops, Tablets and Smartphones

Since 1985, through many different but converging technological discoveries and developments, computing power has increased exponentially, and the size and weight of devices has decreased so much that we have some extremely compact personal devices. The cartoon joke of the time was one manufacturing director saying to the other, 'We have been so successful (at reducing the size of the components) we are going to have to move into a smaller factory!'

At least three other technologies have been required to complete this advancement. Computer screens have been reduced from large cathode ray tubes as in the first television sets, to bright, slim, flat screens. Telephone technology has produced miniature devices for radio signal transmission and receiving devices that we call 'mobiles'. Finally, by combining all of these with space technology and satellites, our mobiles can calculate where we are on the surface of the earth.

So Much Technical Advancement!

So, in the course of about 300 years or 12 human generations since the start of the industrial revolution, after 200,000 years of evolution, technological creativity has produced devices that will fit in your pocket and allow you to see and speak to someone on the other side of the world, and find out information from websites on the Internet that is almost the sum total of all knowledge of the human race.

These achievements have not been made easily; they have been obtained through curiosity, obsession, passion, failure, disappointment, bankruptcy and frustration. Similarly, in the future, advances will only be achieved through commitment, strong leadership, personal discipline, training and knowledge.

Now, every month, in Great Britain, we hear of serious shortcomings in the way we organise ourselves to deliver government, health, education, energy, communication and transport services. Some of these shortcomings affect life and limb; some cost billions of pounds of tax payer's money and some are just highly irritating and annoying.

Lately, cyber attacks have brought down some major information technology (IT) systems, paralysing the systems that use them.

What can be done to make improvements, and in the words of so many politicians and commentators put into effect their plea, 'Lessons must be learned'?

Complacency in the Past

During my career in management consulting, it has been remarkable how many management teams I met accepted that certain practices causing inefficiencies were well known but no one had the time or courage to do anything about them. Sometimes when circumstances demanded that something had to be done, such as a serious quality or cost problem, the company 'troubleshooter' (I knew one known as 'Mr Flapping Coat Tails'; we wore jackets at work in those days) was put on the job because he had seen the problem before. The fact that the problem had reoccurred did not affect his reputation at all; he was the expert and enjoyed the adrenaline rush of 'firefighting'.

When these problems affected customers, the customer services team would be advised, and methods would be introduced to manage the customers' expectations with a helpline. Anyone working in these customer service departments would not be eager for the number of problems to be reduced otherwise they would be out of a job, so there was little incentive to eliminate the causes. Unacceptable situations were just the 'culture of the business we are in'. There was little incentive to improve.

In an ideal world the customer service department would consist of one person sitting by a silent telephone, not unlike that old Carlsberg advert in which the telephone was covered in cobwebs, 'The Dusty Carlsberg Complaints Department'. It can still be viewed on YouTube.

Can These Ideas Be Applied to the National Health Service?

There is an opinion in many businesses and service organisations that the lessons learned in manufacturing for improving quality do not apply in their business. Their business is different. Their business is about people not things. Their business has too many variables for quality control to be applied. Their business deals with living organisms not dead objects, and so on.

This is not so, and I will demonstrate why in this book. Realising that lessons can be learned from other organisations is the major lesson of this book, and the following examples illustrate the power of statistical methods in continuous improvement.

How Times Have Changed: The Power of Statistical Methods

In the last 100 years, manufacturing industry has made great progress to provide us with the things we rely on: cars, aircraft, mobile phones, computing devices, houses, furniture, TVs and so on.

Let me illustrate how times have changed with some personal experiences. I bought my first car in around 1959. It was an Austin Cambridge 10, made in 1939. I think it cost £35 when the monthly wage was about £40. Two experiences stand out. The exhaust fell off on one of its first Sunday outings, much to my future wife's embarrassment. That was repaired. Then, when I had removed and replaced the cylinder head to put in a new gasket, as I was test driving it, a spark plug blew out of its socket, hitting the underside of the bonnet. I soon abandoned it and bought a Lambretta 125 scooter.

These faults rarely happen now.

My next car was an Austin A35, about three years old. The M6 had opened up to Lancashire and we went on a long journey. Going over a Lake District pass the engine overheated, and water from a stream was needed. It turned out that the 'big ends' had worn, and an engine overhaul was needed with 32,000 miles on the clock.

Now, using sophisticated statistical techniques, car engines can last 200,000 miles – 7 times more – and bodywork is guaranteed for 6 years or more.

These are light-hearted anecdotes, but my point is that cars now are so much more reliable and have features that had not been invented when I owned my first cars. Engines now are much more powerful, economic and reliable, and this has been achieved by means of a structured, scientific approach to the improvement process (as well as the basic engineering technology).

It took an American professor, Dr. W. Edwards Deming,[2] advising the Japanese to pioneer these methods of improvement, and the result is that for the last 25 years at least, Japanese manufacturers Honda, Toyota, Nissan and Mazda have topped the league table for vehicle reliability. Many of the techniques that have emerged are well-known terms in business: Kaizen, continuous improvement, statistical process control, Kanban, zero tolerance (for errors) and many more.

However, once the Japanese manufacturers perfected their approach, and their motorcycles and TV sets, then cars, swamped the European marketplace, the British manufacturers could not compete and now have almost all gone out of business. Of the mass volume British vehicle manufacturers, Jaguar and Land Rover, Ford and Vauxhall survive but under foreign ownership. Toyota, Honda and Nissan manufacture in Britain but under Japanese control.

There is one area where British skills are world class: Formula One racing teams such as McLaren have adopted advanced improvement techniques and are world-leading centres of excellence.

What killed off the British manufacturers was their inability to change, and their inability to grasp what continuous improvement and innovation really meant. They were in a competitive market, and customers bought elsewhere because they could buy better products at lower prices. The competition was better and they voted with their feet, do you remember Chapter 3?

These are the reasons why the methods I outline in this book, developed by manufacturing industry, can be used in any service organisation, and will be essential for the NHS to continue to improve: hence the phrase 'continuous improvement'.

The Difficulty of the Task to Improve

Healthcare is a combination of extremely complex chemical and engineering technology rendered to persons at the extremes of their vulnerability by highly trained people who can be at the edge of their limits due to time pressures. Therefore, everyone must apply the most progressive methods to make sure that the simple errors are eliminated and so that the more complex and challenging work can be done effectively to the patient's advantage.

READER EXERCISE

What innovation or change for the better would you like to see in your workplace? How would you propose the idea?

Chapter 6

What This Book Cannot Cover

SUMMARY

There are aspects of the National Health Service (NHS) which can only be improved by government ministers and the directors responsible for the funding and direction of the whole service.

Within the NHS there are a number of issues which need to be considered because of their impact on any work to make improvements:

Issue 1: Do we, the public, the media and politicians, expect too much from what we perceive to be a single organisation of 1.7 million employees?

Issue 2: How should whistle blowers, cover ups and bad press be handled?

Issue 3: Are there too many layers of management?

Issue 4: Will there ever be enough money?

Issue 5: How do we get everyone to understand the continuous improvement process?

Issues 1–4 all involve political strategic direction and are outside the scope of this book, and in consequence it only addresses Issue 5, getting everyone to understand the continuous improvement process.

Issue 1: Organisational Size – Do We Expect Too Much from the NHS?

Although the NHS has many different component parts, in four different regions of the United Kingdom, each one managed, governed or controlled by politicians, civil servants, directors or partners, most lay people perceive it to be a single organisation even though it is not. This could be because we read too many sweeping statements about the service as a whole. Even the smallest dental practice is perceived as being 'part of the NHS' and somehow controlled from above by government.

There are at least three reasons that make the large size of the NHS a cause for not achieving uniformly high standards:

1. The NHS is too big for there never to be some pockets of poor quality somewhere.
2. It is also too big for every employee to have the personal skills and attitudes to deliver excellence.
3. It is so big that finding and re-educating those with the wrong attitudes will be very difficult to achieve, especially if they are in management positions or higher.

It is not difficult to justify these statements numerically. Although the data is always changing, the scale itself is sufficient to justify the comments, not the precise data. I have attempted to get the most accurate numbers here, but I have found that sources differ because of different definitions and dates. For example when counting hospitals, there first has to be a definition of what a hospital is. According to various sources, there are approximately 1532 hospitals,[1] 7600 general practitioner (GP) practices in England,[2] 150,273 qualified medical practitioners,[3] 1.7 million employees (doctors, consultants, nurses, specialists, administrators etc.),[2] and the capabilities of these people are going to range over the full spectrum from excellent to poor. Facilities will age somewhere; techniques will become outmoded somewhere; and patient's demands will exceed supply somewhere.

The skill of managing the service will be to know locally where these weaknesses are, to be able to limit the damage caused and to ensure that the whole service is not castigated because of the mistakes of a few.

To reduce the effect of the large size of the service, as with any very large organisation, every operating unit and every employee must be made accountable to their local community for the quality of the service they provide.

1. The quality of every outcome must be quantified, measured and published at the local level.
2. Errors and unexpected outcomes must be investigated locally and the causes removed to prevent repetition. The saying 'How many babies is a midwife allowed to drop?' is an excellent example of a zero defects approach to patient safety.
3. Every employee must understand, accept and use this approach.
4. The organisation must be led, not micro-managed.

These four points are not revolutionary as they have been fundamental in many manufacturing industries for many years. Those who do not understand the philosophy can perceive them as bureaucratic, expensive and hence 'wasteful at the sharp end'. This is common in those service industries unused to the need to measure the quality of a personally delivered skill.

As many recent events have shown, professionals can make mistakes, and it is how society and their colleagues react to these mistakes that determines whether there will be an improvement or not.

There is a saying in management books 'You can eat an elephant if you divide it into bite-size chunks', and this is a very appropriate metaphor for making improvements in the NHS.

Issue 2: Whistle Blowers, Cover Ups and Bad Press

A fundamental requirement of any successful continuous improvement programme is that all errors are identified, and the root causes are removed. You would not be able to fly safely around the world today if aircraft makers 'brushed mistakes under the carpet'. Excellent standards of service cannot be achieved unless the causes of poor standards are understood and eliminated completely, which is the zero defects or zero tolerance philosophy.

Quality has to be built or planned in to the processes, and the people must be trained to deliver a high-quality service with due regard for whoever is receiving the service. Traditional quality control by inspection is totally inappropriate in healthcare; imagine the ridiculousness of a quality control inspector sitting alongside a medical professional ready to say

'Stop, you are wrong!' High standards of quality must be built into the delivery process by focusing on three factors: training, resources and motivation.

Root causes cannot be identified when there is a cover up. So does this mean that 'whistle blowers' should be encouraged? The simple answer is yes, but the manner and framework of whistle blowing has to be very carefully controlled, otherwise vindictive personal vendettas could prevail. A government paper on blame has been published recently, 'From a Blame Culture to a Learning Culture', 9–10 March 2016.[4]

The media will always hunt for examples of poor performance, look for someone to blame and shout for that person's 'scalp'. Although this is negative and highly embarrassing for all concerned, in a well-run organisation it would happen less and less because habitual poor performers would have been weeded out by the performance evaluation system.

However, the media could be a powerful force for good if, whenever an example of bad practice was found, the newspaper or TV programme maker was obliged to find out from the well-performing hospitals the method used to avoid or prevent that type of error from happening. A balanced report would then be produced, for example 'This is what happened at X and this is how organisation Y stops such events occurring'.

Issue 3: Layers of Management

In its present form the NHS has many layers of operational and political managers in both controlling and advisory positions inside and outside the direct action. If the NHS were to be recreated, how many of these 'non-productive overheads' would be considered absolutely essential to the smooth running of the service? I will let the reader answer that one.

Issue 4: Finance

With a service 'free at the point of delivery' to an ever more needful population, there is never going to be enough money to treat the increasingly more exotic ailments that all of us can succumb to. All the NHS can do is make sure it does the best with what it has, but how would that judgement be made?

Issue 5: How Do We Get Everyone to Understand the Continuous Improvement Processes?

Understanding the improvement process involves

- Understanding the processes that need improving, that is the patient journey
- Understanding the process of continuous improvement
- Understanding the problem-solving process

This is the subject of this book, read on.

Chapter 7

Quality, Quality Assurance and Continuous Improvement

SUMMARY

The meanings of these terms within healthcare are explained. The concept of continuous improvement is introduced and connects these terms to audits and inspections.

In well-run healthcare units, inspections should not be necessary; the management should know the status of quality and have its own improvement plan.

Definitions of Quality

There are many definitions of the word 'quality'. It is used as a noun as in 'of a superior quality' meaning 'of a higher standard'; or as in 'the quality of a service' meaning how the nature of that service is measured. It can also be used as an adjective as in 'a quality service' meaning a service of a high standard, quality inferring superiority. Another definition is 'the degree of excellence of a thing', a form of ranking one item against another.

So when it comes to goods and services many people have different perceptions of the precise meaning of the word. In fact, I have often advised clients not to use the word but to find a word that is more precise for their own situation, such as value for money, hassle free, fast, reliable and so on.

One UK paint manufacturer has brought a new phrase into British English: 'It does exactly what it says on the tin'.

The field of quality assurance concerns itself with ensuring a consistent standard of quality of goods and services to a specification that has been agreed between the supplier and the customer. In healthcare this would be between the service provider and the patient.

There are two ways for this process of providing a service to be delivered. The first is the best one where the provider gives the patient exactly what is needed (within accepted clinical restraints). In quality assurance terms, this is called 'being customer driven'. The second is where the provider only provides what they want to provide (or are able to provide); this is called being producer driven and is not considered to be a quality service.

Another consideration is 'low cost'. Low cost does not mean poor quality, and high cost does not mean good quality. If the low-cost product or service gives complete customer satisfaction then it is an excellent quality provision. If a high-cost product or service does not give customer satisfaction then it is of poor quality, no matter how good the after-sales service is. In Table 7.1 I have set out four combinations of a customer's opinion of each combination of cost and reliability, reliability in this context meaning 'of a consistent standard'. The style of this type of chart is known as a 2×2 matrix, producing four different combinations, discussed further in Chapter 20. Box 1 low cost, low reliability is what many people would call 'cheap and nasty'. Box 2 high cost and unreliable would be a 'rip off'. Box 3 low cost and reliable would be a 'bargain'. And finally, Box 4 high cost and reliable would be a 'prestigious' or 'luxury' item or service.

READER EXERCISE

Think of your own personal examples of goods and services that you would put in each of the four boxes in the matrix.

It could be argued that as far as the NHS is concerned, because it is free at the point of delivery, then it does not fit the model in Table 7.1 – but it does. It costs the nation £120 billion each year (about £2000 per person), and to manage this cost every clinical procedure is 'costed' for budgetary purposes. The patient pays through his/her taxes. In an insurance based system, the insurance companies will be looking for 'value for money'.

Summarising these concepts, most quality assurance professionals would define quality as 'goods and services that provide complete customer satisfaction, from start to the finish of the service or the life of the product'.

Table 7.1   Quality and Cost

	Unreliable (Poor Quality) ↓	*Reliable (High Quality)* ↓
High Cost →	Box 2 Rip off	Box 4 Prestigious or luxury
Low Cost →	Box 1 Cheap and nasty	Box 3 A bargain

Taking the understanding of 'quality' further, there are national professional bodies that promote this subject.

The American Society for Quality

In the United States, the American Society for Quality[1] defines quality as

'A subjective term for which each person or sector has its own definition. In technical usage, quality can have two meanings: (1) the characteristics of a product or service that bear on its ability to satisfy stated or implied needs; (2) a product or service free of deficiencies. According to Joseph Juran, quality means "fitness for use"; according to Philip Crosby, it means "conformance to requirements"'.

The UK Chartered Quality Institute

The Chartered Quality Institute (CQI) is the United Kingdom's nationally recognised professional body for maintaining the standards for those people engaged in managing and implementing quality standards at work. It has defined quality as 'an outcome – a characteristic of a product or service provided to a customer, and the hallmark of an organisation which has satisfied all its customers'.[2]

The institute then divided the achievement of these aims by seeking answers to these questions under three headings shown in Table 7.2.

Table 7.2 Are Sound Quality Standards Being Achieved?

Heading	Question
Governance	1. Is management intent defined through the organisation's policies and required ways of working? 2. Are these policies and ways of working fit for purpose with respect to all stakeholders' needs?
Assurance	3. Are the defined policies and ways of working effectively implemented? 4. Do the activities produce the desired outcomes (for all stakeholders)?
Improvement	5. Is there a culture of evaluation and improvement to address risks, failures, non-conformances and inefficiency/waste?

The CQI has to set out definitions such as these for all types of organisations, and the language and jargon might seem strange to anyone working in a profession like the NHS that has its own language and jargon.

However, Lord Darzi has helped bring the NHS and the CQI definitions closer with his own explanation. Professor Lord Darzi, Chair of Surgery at Imperial College London, was commissioned by the government in 2006 to review the state of the NHS.

Lord Darzi's Definition of Quality

Lord Darzi, holder of the Paul Hamlyn Chair of Surgery at Imperial College London, the Royal Marsden Hospital and the Institute of Cancer Research, in his reports in 2007[3] and 2008[4] defined quality for the NHS as comprising three dimensions:

- Safety (avoiding harm from the care that is intended to help)
- Effectiveness (aligning care with science and ensuring efficiency)
- Patient experience (including patient-centeredness, timeliness and equity).

'An effective quality management system includes quality control (to keep sound processes reliable on a daily basis), quality improvement (to decrease variation within and among NHS organisations so that the best becomes the norm) and quality planning (especially fostering innovative care models that can deliver better outcomes at lower cost)'.

This definition for healthcare professionals covers the same concepts as those in the CQI definition.

Quality Management and Quality Assurance

The CQI describes quality management as all those coordinated activities that are required to direct and control an organisation with regard to quality.

Quality assurance is that part of quality management focused on providing confidence that quality requirements will be fulfilled.

Relating quality management to Lord Darzi's definition puts the question 'who' in front of each element, for example who (in your part of the organisation) is responsible for the safety, the effectiveness and the patient experience?

Looking at this from another angle, ask who sets the standards, who monitors the achievement of those standards and who decides where improvements must be made.

The effective organisation should know immediately whether the correct standard has been delivered and if not, the action to be taken to prevent a reoccurrence. Usually the provider carrying out the work knows whether standards have been achieved and should be able to take the corrective action immediately. It should not be necessary to wait for an investigation to be carried out or an enquiry to be held before corrective and preventative action is taken. Corrective action is putting right what has gone wrong; preventative action is action taken to prevent that problem occurring again.

One argument against this self-policing, self-improvement approach is that it often ends up with an internal cover up. This can be avoided with good quality assurance supervision. In the major quality system standard ISO 9001,[5] used by industry throughout the world, one of the first checks the auditor makes when auditing a self-policing organisation is to look at the methods and results of the self-auditing system and the way in which trends are monitored and acted upon. Only when adverse operational results are found would the supervising body 'drill down' and audit (or inspect) a representative sample of the control procedures. A self-policing system needs a fully traceable set of improvement records.

Quality Management Systems

There are international standards for quality management systems (QMSs), and trained auditors from approved organisations carry out inspections or audits to determine whether the organisation is doing what it says it does in its documented QMS. These international standards define a QMS as a documented set of policies, processes and procedures required for planning and execution in the core business area of an organisation (i.e. areas that can impact the organisation's ability to meet customer requirements); ISO 9001:2015 is an example of a QMS standard.[5]

Referring back to Lord Darzi's definition of quality for the NHS, if ISO 9001 were to be applied, every organisation should have a documented QMS that describes how the organisation implements the requirements of the relevant standard for quality. Only when all of this is written down, agreed, approved and communicated to everyone will a sensible audit of how well it is implemented be carried out and reported.

A Practical Example: Pressure or Bed Sores

All of this theory can be simply explained with an example.

A typical QMS would state, in a manual, how a particular activity would be carried out. If it was the monitoring of bed sores it would define how they would be counted, what action would be taken to assist the patient, how the results would be monitored, how trends would be reported and whether any action that had been taken to prevent their reoccurrence had been effective. Most hospitals should already have this data.

For a full QMS, senior management would decide what other types of event needed to be similarly monitored, such as infection outbreaks, re-admissions, falls and so on, extending the standard methods to every significant aspect of the organisation's work.

The new NHS Safety Thermometer defines most of this, and in time a sound improvement system should develop.[6]

If bed sores have been completely eliminated on a ward, regular counting would not be necessary, and the infrequent occurrence would be reported as an exceptional event; some people call this a 'Red Flag' event, Red Flag meaning something that must receive immediate attention. This exceptional event should be measured on the basis of how long has it been since the last one? In statistical terms it can be counted as 'time between failures', similar to the safety criterion 'time since last fatal accident'.

Having prepared a document, to go into the QMS, describing this monitoring process, the hospital or nursing home does not need an outside inspector to tell the manager whether it is being carried out – the local manager should know, and as an extra safeguard a trained internal auditor can be delegated to carry out internal audits. But also, the nursing staff will be trained in the system and will know whether or not the correct methods are being followed. In an ideal world the auditor should always find that the procedures are being followed. It would be a serious non-conformance to find otherwise. The expression 'non-conformance' might be new to many readers – it means any situation when the correct results or outcomes have not been achieved. However, most professional specialisms will have their own equivalent word. This is the basis of a sound quality assurance system and should be standard practice.

The causes for this type of occurrence and procedural omission would be overwork, slack supervision, laziness or incompetence.

Furthermore, in a well-run unit with a good QMS it should not be necessary to be inspected by an organisation such as the Care Quality Commission (CQC), where an external inspector does a lot of checking of work; all that should be necessary would be an audit of the internal QMS procedures. Under these circumstances, when the CQC finds a non-compliance it means the internal quality assurance methods have failed.

Many quality assurance specialists would probably agree with me that the need for an inspection organisation such as the CQC is an admission of failure because the providers being inspected are not able to assure the quality of the services they provide.

There is a principle that is held in many quality assurance situations that any worker should have the knowledge and resources to know whether they have produced work of an adequate quality and they have the authority to call a halt and ask for help to rectify the situation regardless of their status in the organisation.

Another Practical Example: Nil by Mouth

In Chapter 4 I described two incidents where 'Nil by Mouth' disciplines were breached at two different hospitals several years apart, evidence to me of a possible systemic weakness throughout the United Kingdom. On this evidence I must assume that this is a common failing, notwithstanding the possibility that a large proportion of hospital wards have good systems, and I would like to use these two instances to illustrate how a good QMS would help reduce the risk of this procedure being overlooked. Reports in 2014 by the King's Fund[7] say there are 140,000 beds in UK hospitals, so it is very worthwhile to have a national standard for this aspect of patient safety.

The classic quality assurance approach to this would be as follows.

There would be a standard approach to visible signage when a patient is 'Nil by Mouth', say, a sign or board by the patient's bed. In the hospital standards manual (if there isn't one there should be), the exact way this is done would be described. As well as this, everyone who gives out food and drink would be trained in the importance of knowing whether a patient is Nil by Mouth or not. In no way should anyone rely on the patient remembering their status and having to refuse food or drink. Having done this the system is set up. After time it is possible that a breach will occur, but that breach has to be discovered, hopefully without having a dangerous effect on the patient. This must be formally reported and documented because, without doing so, no one will know whether it is an isolated incident or not. In quality assurance terms it is a 'non-conformance', something that should not have happened.

In the event that someone does break the Nil by Mouth instruction it must be recorded, it should not be covered up or swept under the carpet; nor should the perpetrator be punished, otherwise how would the true extent of similar breaches be known? The purpose of the QMS is to give assurance that the correct procedures will be carried out and that undesirable events will be prevented.

Having recorded the breach an investigation must be made to establish how it happened and steps taken and recorded to remove that particular cause, either by retraining the offender or putting special restrictions on food and drink. This is known as preventative action.

Why Is This Paperwork Necessary?

First, it reduces the probability of serious post-operative complications, and additionally it makes the investigation of any post-operative complication easier because it rules out food or drink in the digestive tract as a cause (shooting yourself in the foot versus real problems).

Secondly, when a quality inspection/audit is carried out it demonstrates to the inspector/auditor that the correct patient safety procedures are being carried out and that action to prevent reoccurrence (continuous improvement) is being taken. It provides an audit trail.

Continuous Improvement

Continuous improvement is a philosophy in which the organisation is never satisfied with the status quo. It is about everyone having the attitude 'we can always do better'. However, a continuous improvement approach to work needs strong leadership, and it works better when everyone follows agreed, set principles and procedures. It is about finding out how to do things more simply and hence faster, or at less expense or with better outcomes or combinations of all three. But it must be applied to the whole patient treatment process, it is no good cutting corners at the beginning only to incur more cost later on. In fact, it is often found that taking more time at the start of any piece of work saves much more time at the end, providing a net gain. Get the preparation right and the job is usually easier and more successful. The long-established name of this philosophy is Total Quality.

Audits and Inspections in Continuous Improvement

Having a project management approach to continuous improvement (Chapter 14) will increase the chances of success. Through its very formality the project will be perceived as being important, records will be kept, progress will be monitored and reviewed and it is more likely that the findings will be implemented. Once implemented the 'system' will have learned and changed. The improved knowledge will no longer be the personal property of individual investigators, and the 'intelligence' of the organisation will have been strengthened. This is an important aspect of the culture of the organisation – all knowledge must be shared and must never become the jealously guarded property of an individual.

These formal records will also demonstrate to external inspectors that a structured, focused programme of improvement is in place. Modern quality management standards such as ISO 9001 have several requirements relevant to this chapter. The first is that the people in any organisation, no matter how large or small, should regularly check whether they are following the correct processes, and second, they should check that they are achieving the appropriate standards for the outcomes (internal audits). This should not be months after some disaster, but on a regular basis. Various sayings spring to mind – 'Prevention is better than cure', 'It was like shutting the stable door after the horse had bolted' and so on.

When it is discovered that either correct processes or correct outcomes are not being achieved, corrective and preventive actions are required.

Corrective action puts right what was found to be at fault. Suppose the wrong dose of medication has been prescribed for a patient, they have taken that dosage and it is on the patient's record for repeats. Corrective action would be to check whether the patient had suffered any long-term effect, bad or good; to respond to that finding; then to correct the dosage on the record.

Preventive action would be to find out all the possible causes of the error and to put changes in place to stop that fault happening ever again.

On subsequent inspections or audits, the QMS inspectors/auditors would want to see, from the records, demonstration that both corrective and preventive actions had been taken. This is the audit trail they are looking for and it is a plus for the organisation being audited; it should not be penalized for the original error, although for some errors, formal disciplinary procedures have to be followed.

An independent assessment of the quality of any work is always a good thing; it ensures that standards are being maintained. Without that independent second opinion, standards will slip or be abused as happened with Dr. Shipman who was found guilty in 2000 of murdering 15 elderly patients in Hyde, Manchester. Later investigations by the Shipman Inquiry[8] in 2002 have decided that he murdered 215 patients at least.

We should not get too hung up on the difference in meaning between the words 'inspection' and 'audit'. In broad terms an inspection looks at the quality of the work outputted, whereas an audit looks to see whether systems and procedures are being followed. Having reviewed all the different meanings and uses of the words 'audit' and 'inspection', I have come to the conclusion that they are on a spectrum of peer reviews carried out by what I shall call 'checkers'. Pure audit at one end of the spectrum would examine only the manner in which the systems and procedures are being used as in an ISO 9001 Quality Systems audit. Pure inspection at the other end of the spectrum is simply the close examination of a piece of work against the standard expected of it.

Whatever way the words 'audit' and 'inspection' are used, whenever either is carried out the terms of reference should be clearly documented and agreed by both parties so that they understand what is being examined, why and how it will be reported and acted upon. The final report should praise the good points and highlight the inadequacies. The inspectors or the auditors should not leave the place of work of those people whose work they have checked without agreeing the findings in full at a documented 'closing meeting'. At this meeting those inspected should have the 'right to reply', for example to find missing records. It is wrong for the checkers to spring a surprise on those checked at a later date. Before leaving, both parties should also agree a timed action plan to remedy any shortcomings that have been found. The plan should be signed and dated by both parties.

There are times when there is a strong disagreement between the checker and those being checked. These disagreements must be aired at the time of the check and a plan agreed to resolve the differences of opinion, often by reference to a higher authority.

When the very future of an organisation is at stake, as when it is put into 'special measures', a clear, strong, documented action plan will be needed. Every deficiency should be listed and both corrective and preventative action put in place.

If the deficiencies that have been found are serious enough, the checker should arrange a return visit after an agreed timescale to review the improvements that have been made. The organisation has no choice, and should the director in charge decide to ignore an item and do something else it will count very badly on a re-assessment visit.

It has been reported by the CQC[9] that of 1649 core services at NHS acute trusts, inspected as of 31 December 2016, 701 either were inadequate or required improvement. When 433 re-inspections, to 31 January 2017, were carried out, of 1649 core services within the total of 136 acute non-specialist trusts, the rating of 65 had deteriorated and 225 showed no change. This shows that much has yet to be learned about the implementation of quality improvement, but the CQC is showing the way.

It can be seen from this that external audits or inspections provide an important input to any organisation's improvement programme. They provide a list of opportunities that must be managed, and Chapter 22, 'Multiple Project Management', shows how this can be done.

Kaizen

Many of the methods described in this book are standard parts of a continuous improvement programme, which the Japanese call 'Kaizen' as described by Masaaki Imai in his 1986 book on the subject.[10] Recently it has been used under the title 'marginal gains' by many organisations including British Cycling, who have transformed the sport to be the best in the world.

In 2002 these methods were adopted and championed in healthcare by the Virginia Mason Institute in Seattle,[11] and it is now a world leader in the application of continuous improvement to the field.

Kaizen means gradual, unending improvement, doing little things better, setting and achieving ever-higher standards. It is a philosophy for working and includes the philosophies shown in the following table (Table 7.3).

Six Sigma

Six Sigma is a set of statistical quality management techniques that is most effective in the manufacturing industry. It uses measuring techniques to assess the variability of products coming off a production line. Once the variability of the process has been established, the process is re-engineered to reduce the variation making the product more consistent and repeatable. In healthcare it is most likely to be used in the production to a specification of such items as breast implants, artificial joints and medication (pills and lotions), improving their reliability.

It has recently been reported in *BMJ* (*British Medical Journal*) Open[12] that an investigation into 489 metal-on-metal hip joints, 71 requiring further replacement, 'a significant number … were found to be manufactured out of specification'. The manufacturer disputed the findings. This would be an ideal application for Six Sigma methods when the manufacturers and the researchers share the findings to improve the way these artificial joints are specified and production controlled.

Table 7.3   Elements of Kaizen

Kaizen Element	Practical Aspects
Top management commitment	Managers at all levels must understand the principles of Kaizen and be prepared to learn and apply them.
Problem solving	The ability to recognise a problem and prevent it from happening again.
Customer orientation and satisfaction (internal and external)	All activities must be focused on the patient and the internal customer supplier relationships (Chapter 9).
Zero defects	Errors are not acceptable, anywhere.
Quality improvement	Never being content with current level of achievement.
Suggestion schemes	Ideas for improvement are encouraged and responded to.
Total productive maintenance	Increasing the productivity of plant and equipment with a modest investment in maintenance.
Just in time	Reducing queues, waiting times and surplus supplies of stock.
Productivity improvement	Everyone becoming more effective through the elimination of waste.
Discipline in the workplace	Correcting behavioural deficiencies and ensuring adherence to established company rules.
New product development	Having a planned systematic programme of innovation.
Systems improvement	Constantly reviewing methods of working.
Process redesign	Analysing existing processes and looking for improvements.

Chapter 8

Dealing with Complaints

SUMMARY

Explains what complaints are, how to handle them, and how to use them for quality improvement. They should be collected together in a register, analysed for common features, and action should be taken to prevent reoccurrence.

Background

In the Care Quality Commission (CQC) report of 14 October 2015, 'The State of Healthcare and Adult Social Care in England', it states the Health and Social Care Information Centre (HSCIC) as quoting that the number of written complaints in a year numbered 207,000, over 500 per day.[1] What a wealth of information that must contain for patient care improvement if it could be looked at positively and not defensively!

This aspect of healthcare must be one of the most contentious to manage at all levels, but why contentious? Probably because of the very variable expectations of patients, the wide variation in the quality/standard of the service provided, the possible lack of a standard against which performance can be measured and the very personal relationship between a patient and their general practitioner (GP) or provider. Should we all be eternally grateful that the government has provided this free service from cradle to grave and just take it as it comes, or, because we pay our taxes (or insurance) should we expect a smooth, efficient, professional, fault-free one? Everyone will have a different attitude to this, but from an efficiency point of view important information can be gathered regarding duplicated phone calls, wasted journeys and visits, and even duplicated tests when records have gone missing.

There is a fear in healthcare that admitting to mistakes or malpractice will prove costly for the organisation and the individual concerned, and this fear leads to denial and cover up. In turn, this becomes the most serious barrier to making improvements, dealing with the very small proportion of people who are evil, incompetent, lazy or both, who give the whole National Health Service (NHS) a bad name due to the publicity received in the popular newspapers.

The very varied nature of healthcare complaints can be explained in Figure 8.1, in which I have shown what I have called a spectrum of poor healthcare quality.

On the left of the spectrum are the day-to-day nuisances; on the extreme right are the most serious, usually malicious, events. In between are examples of increasingly serious types of poor healthcare.

On one hand it is self-evident that as the types of poor quality get more serious there is a greater chance of litigation and financial cost to the

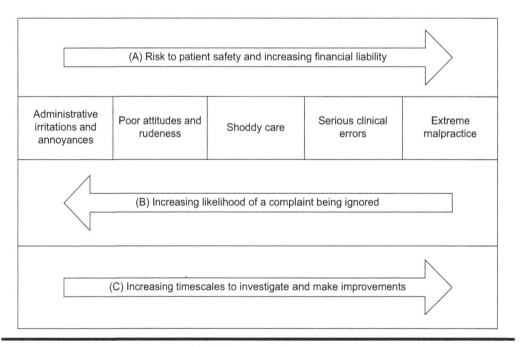

Figure 8.1 A spectrum of poor healthcare quality.

organisation (Arrow A). Procedures to handle the most serious of these will become very bureaucratic and legalistic.

On the other hand those minor types on the left of the spectrum are less litigatious and less likely to have serious financial consequences. So will these types be considered less important and ignored (Arrow B)?

The question is, however, are the faults on the left of this spectrum the base of the Bird's safety triangle described in Chapter 1 and those on the right equivalent to the fatalities at the apex of that triangle? If they are then by reducing the incidence of the faults to the left, would the number of fatalities decrease?

Another factor suggested by this spectrum is that it is possible, but not inevitable, that the timescales for investigating the most serious examples of poor quality will take the longest to investigate, feed back into the systems and implement procedures to prevent reoccurrence.

The conclusion from this is that complaint systems will tend to ignore the types of poor quality on the left of the spectrum.

Given that in many situations the final decisions, especially investment ones, are made by the accountants, then surely it will be when complaints cost money that changes will be made. As long as the inefficiencies do not impact on the operating accounts they could continue to be ignored. Many other businesses have this problem.

In the world of business it has been recognised that customer complaints are very important feedback for the providers of goods and services, especially in a competitive environment. In the book *A Complaint Is a Gift*, Janelle Barlow and Claus Moller make the assertion that complaints are 'not annoyances to be dodged, denied, or buried but are instead valuable pieces of feedback'.[2]

Even as far back as 1993 it has been reported[3] that Virginia Bottomley, the Minister of State for Health, had declared that complaints are 'jewels to be treasured'.

What Is a Complaint?

A complaint arises when a customer (or patient) is dissatisfied with the goods or services provided. To be dissatisfied, the customer's expectations will not have been met. Dissatisfaction ranges widely from the most severe when goods or services are totally at fault, to the minor irritations that sometimes spoil an otherwise brilliant service. Because everyone's expectations are different, especially in healthcare, there often is a wide variation in the quality of service offered and considered acceptable by the provider and what in the patient's opinion is acceptable at the point of receipt.

This might appear to be stating the obvious, but in many situations the complainant often gets the response 'Why are you complaining, it is the same for everyone?', implying the concern is the same for all.

Typical comments from dissatisfied patients are

'It didn't work'.
'They made a mistake'.
'It took too long'.
'You/he/she never said that would happen'.
'I didn't know it would cost that much'.
'He/she was so rude, I felt ill for days'.
'She was so rude, I was frightened to say anything'.
'It was three days late'.
'I didn't have a clue what was going on'.
'My holiday was spoilt because ….'
'I waited for three hours at the ….'
And the classic,
'The operation was a success but unfortunately the patient died'.

There must be many more examples of complaints, some very serious, others appearing quite trivial, but often those trivial complaints are a sign of some more serious problem.

In the early days of ISO 9001 the Quality Assurance Standard there was a company where the first stage in the customer complaint process was to decide whether the complaint was 'justified' – had the customer followed the instructions correctly or expected too much of the service? The supplier response being 'Sorry it's not our fault', translated this meant 'Go away you are wasting our time'. Often in these examples the provider has not been very clear in the instructions provided for the customer.

In another example involving a travel company selling package holidays, a director told me that they could not start to compensate every customer who complained because it would open the flood gates, everyone would find something to complain about and want cash.

The quality manager of a large motor manufacturer once reported that every time someone was dissatisfied with their car they told an average 50 people, whereas satisfied customers don't often tell many people how good their car is. Bad news travels further and faster than good news.

In the 1990s, the early days of personal computing, if the software misbehaved it seemed as though the suppliers often tried to put the blame on the user so that after that, if something went wrong, the user usually asked themselves 'What have I done wrong?' The software houses put out software without adequate testing and in my experience, rarely took ownership of the problems.

So in the world of continuous improvement, where suppliers are looking for increasing customer satisfaction, all feedback from customers is extremely valuable. Some feedback is positive, and the rest is some form of complaint.

Some complaints are very serious while others are irritations; however, how many irritations are needed before the customer goes elsewhere? Except that with the NHS the customer can't go elsewhere.

How many people complain to their GP or their dentist? The fear of antagonising your health professional stops a lot of feedback that could be very informative.

The simple examples of administrative niggles in Chapter 4, '1% Better at 1000 Things', describing how people are prepared to put up with poor service, are trivial ones, but I am sure they are indicative of greater problems. If the complaint is not made then the manager of the service will never know of the dissatisfaction. Moreover, perhaps 10 other patients are also holding back about the same thing – there is then a more serious problem, but nothing will ever be done about it because they all kept quiet for being thought ungrateful or fear of being shouted down.

There was an example of this in the chemical industry. The company's products were being shipped across the world, and an example arose where there was a faulty drum of the product caused by damage in transit. Because it was only one drum, the local overseas manager replaced it out of stock and did not report back to the UK headquarters. Unknown to him, similar one-off faults were occurring in many other countries, and had each one been reported back it would have been seen that there was a relatively serious problem. It is important to know about the smallest faults, and this drives the 1% better at 1000 things philosophy.

The point is that every complaint is extremely valuable to the organisation, and because of this, if a patient has a complaint they should be encouraged to complain and thanked for doing it. Yes, thanked for complaining.

In some situations complaints are intercepted before they reach the people who should know. At the end of one package holiday the representative asked the holiday makers to fill in a satisfaction questionnaire and to hand it back to her when complete. So would unfavourable reviews get back to headquarters? I doubt it.

The Two Stages of a Complaint

Instead of using the word customers I shall refer to patients, and that would include their representatives, carers and relatives.

Ideally there should always be two stages of action to a patient complaint; the first stage (A) is to ensure that the patient is made comfortable, happy and healthy, all adverse effects are treated. In some organisations the company representative is empowered to recompense the customer over and above replacing the faulty article or repeating the service, for example '£15 for the inconvenience Sir/Madam'. But today that would be difficult and not be appropriate to the NHS.

After that, in many organisations the system often falls down; the issue is not reported to a central register, which is stage B. There will be no corporate knowledge of the type and size of the complaints, and senior management will never know what needs to be improved or in what priority order.

Let us look at these stages in turn.

The steps in processing a complaint usually are, in stage A, making the patient happy:

- Acknowledge the complaint, give it a reference number from a central complaints register.
- Apologise and thank the patient for bringing it to your attention.
- Establish the facts (without annoying the complainant) and record them. (Do not be defensive, accept what the complainant is saying without criticism.)
- (Sometimes it is necessary, say if there has been a personal injury or worse, to follow an emergency routine and immediately escalate the complaint to a more senior person).
- Immediately take containment action if it is suspected that other patients could be affected.
- Satisfy the patient, no matter what it takes, and confirm that they are happy. If they are not happy the recipient must escalate the complaint immediately to a 'higher authority'.

- Document and report the facts in a complaints register.
- That would be the end of stage A.

For stage B, during which analysis and future preventive action is taken,

- Forward the complaint records to an appropriate person for analysis. They should then put them in the ongoing improvement programme.
- Check again that the problem will not affect any more patients.
- Determine the root causes (see Chapter 16).
- Take action to stop the problem reoccurring.
- Check that the problem does not reoccur.

These stages should be self-explanatory, and although the general principles will be the same, organisations will manage themselves differently according to the nature of their work.

Recording a Complaint

As part of the organisation's quality planning, there should be a prepared set of guidelines for taking and responding to different complaints usually documented as a complaint form and a complaints register.

The larger the organisation the more organised the system should be to allow for careful analysis of the complaints and planning prioritised improvement action. In most organisations an electronic database can be created to analyse the types and costs of the complaints, but at the start, a good paper system will help to design the system and get it moving.

The procedures for responding to a customer complaint are an essential part of every quality management system.

NHS UK Complaints Policy and Procedures

An example of the way in which complaints are now being handled in the NHS is typified by a document, the 'NHS England Complaints Policy', published in July 2016 by NHS England.[4] Being a policy document it sets out the principles that every part of NHS England should apply to patient complaints. The UK Patients Association has also published in 2013 'Good Practice Standards for NHS Complaints Handling'.[5]

Both of these documents describe how stage A of the patient complaints procedure previously described should be handled, but it appears from the policy document that every individual healthcare unit is left to decide the exact manner and style of how the various elements of the complaint should be documented to record all of the information that is vital for analysis and continuous improvement. There is a need for best practice to be identified and disseminated across the United Kingdom.

One-Off Complaints and Complaint Trends

As Barlow and Moller say, 'Every complaint is a gift'. The system must respond to every complaint according to its seriousness and frequency in a planned, managed and pre-determined way. Some complaints will be a 'one-off', while others will be part of an ongoing trend that is already being monitored. The organisation should either already have a plan for dealing with the complaint as in the case of a known trend, or create a plan on learning about a new one-off.

In some cases, a patient might be happy with an apology and assurances that changes had been made to prevent it happening again. In other cases, medical procedures might have to be carried out to correct some irregularity in which case the patient might expect compensation.

Normally these complaints are coded by type, and an analysis is carried out to plan which problems to put into the continuous improvement programme, but this programme will only be effective if all instances are recorded, and that is not always done.

Internal Complaints

Another concept that many people have difficulty with is the idea that there are 'internal customers and suppliers'.

Any professional might write or dictate notes or a letter for someone else to enter onto the system. If the 'typist', 'secretary' or 'data-entry clerk' cannot understand the writing or the diction, that is an internal complaint to the professional. It is an opportunity for improvement.

If a laboratory is slow reporting results, then that is an internal complaint; it can be measured too, how late, how often late.

If hospitals beds are mechanically or electronically unreliable that is an opportunity for an internal customer complaint. The grapevine probably knows about the extent, but proper reports would quantify the problems.

The barrier to all of these different internal inefficiencies is the loyalty between workmates illustrated by 'I don't want to get them into trouble', even though there are opportunities for improvement.

Dealing with these types of issues will be described in subsequent chapters.

Summary

To summarise,

- All complaints must be recorded in a complaints register.
- The complainant must be responded to until they are totally satisfied.
- The complaint must be thoroughly investigated.
- The problem must be contained.
- The complaints register must be used as a source of topics to be used in a continuous improvement programme.

READER EXERCISE

Do you know what the system is for registering and responding to customer complaints in your place of work? Does it match up to the points made in this chapter?

Chapter 9

Work Processes, the Critical Path and the Chain of Quality

SUMMARY

Work can be speeded up by analysing the steps in the whole process (or procedure), especially when the work crosses departmental boundaries. Finding the longest sequence of tasks will reveal the critical path which can then be subject to modification and refinement.

What Is a Work Process?

All work is a process or a series of processes carried out by trained people, by a machine set up to do a job or by a computer programmed to receive and produce information.

No matter how impersonal and boring it sounds, every process (and by definition every workplace) has 'inputs' and 'outputs' as shown in Figure 9.1.

Within most processes there are many single steps, where the output of one step is the input to the next step.

In professional services, such as any healthcare provider, competent work will only be achieved by trained people who are adequately motivated; given the appropriate resources, correct information and materials; and using reliable, capable equipment.

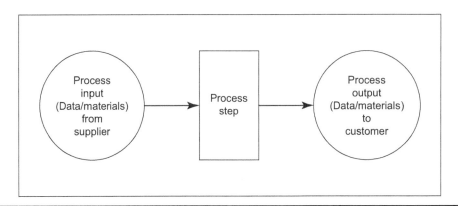

Figure 9.1   A process step.

In this sense, capable means 'able to carry out the task expected'; for example, a plastic picnic knife will not do the job of a scalpel (ability); you cannot measure the time of a 100-metre race with a mantle clock (accuracy); and if a job takes 50 seconds you cannot expect to complete 10 items in any less than 500 seconds (capacity). These examples are glaringly obvious, but in practice the capability is much more subtle and less easy to determine. In a hard-pressed organisation, incapable and or under-capacity resources are often pushed to their limit to attempt to squeeze the last drop out of what is available. This in turn leads to over-work and mistakes.

Curing Patients Is a Process: 'The Patient's Journey'

The patient's journey is the process that any patient goes through, from pre-senting themselves to the first professional, to the final outcome of recovery or otherwise. When a patient is referred by a general practitioner (GP) to a hospital specialist or any healthcare provider it is often only the patient who 'sees' the whole process; the healthcare professionals only know the steps that each one of them is involved in. In fact, because so many steps are compartmentalized, it is often difficult for any single professional to know the full detail of every step a patient moves through. However, to study con-tinuous improvement it is necessary to consider the total process from start to finish, hence the expression popular 30 years ago, 'Total Quality'.

If the reader is wondering why process mapping is referred to so much in reports on the National Health Service (NHS), it is because within the overall patient experience the diagnosis, treatment and care of each person is a col-lection of processes.

The basic process for healthcare is shown in Figure 9.2. It is short and quick and is what might happen should you visit the dentist.

The longer process shown in Figure 9.3 is one that would apply in my home region should a patient present with symptoms that need referral to a specialist in a hospital. In early 2017 every referral from a GP is now passed to a triage unit for a decision to decide which specialist unit should see the patient. This has now introduced further delays into what was already a long and slow process. I have estimated that in this process there are five points where the patient has to either wait for an appointment to be given out, usually by letter, wait until the day of the appointment or wait for laboratory test results or interpretation of a scan. Fortunately, patients suspected of having cancer will be fast tracked.

Surely there is scope for improvement here?

Patient Expectations

Whenever a person presents themselves to a healthcare professional the process is started and the patient expects, both at each stage and across the whole process,

- To be treated courteously and quickly at a speed relative to the seriousness of the ailment
- The ailment to be diagnosed correctly, first time
- The prognosis to be explained clearly
- Suitable treatment to be given quickly
- The treatment to work 'in a reasonable time', or
- If the prognosis is terminal, to be treated with compassion and dignity
- The speedy and error free administration of the healthcare journey

This might appear to be stating the obvious but in any project involving continuous improvement it is good to go back to basic aims.

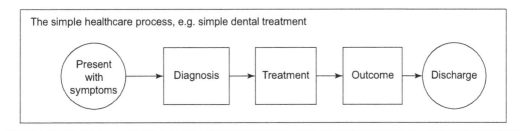

Figure 9.2   The patient's journey.

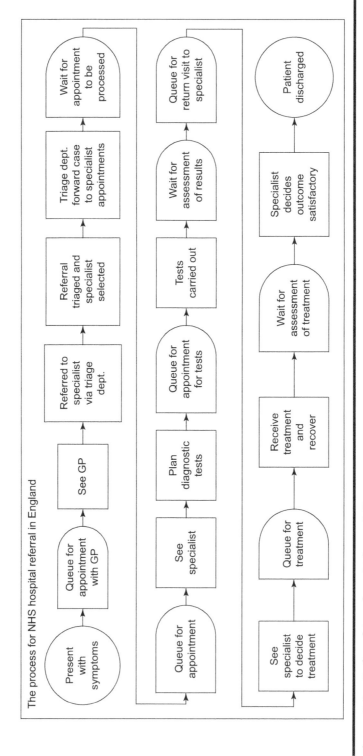

Figure 9.3 Referral to a hospital specialist.

Poor service, therefore, is the opposite of the aforementioned criteria:

- Slow service
- Discourteous behaviour
- Incorrect diagnosis
- Incorrect treatment
- Tardiness and errors in the administration

All of these will lead to wasted time, prolonged pain and disability, embarrassment, unwanted side effects and even unnecessary death.

The aim of the health service is to put each patient through this process as quickly and as successfully as possible. In the simplest of cases this process applies to every specialty – dentists, GPs, physiotherapists, psychologists, psychiatrists and so on. Within each stage of this top-level process there are sub-processes that use such a wide range of skills and departments that moving the patient along from start to finish quickly requires very slick cooperation between specialisms.

To illustrate this point before moving on to the theoretical explanations, the following example shows how a patient can experience rapid, effective treatment from starting at a GP surgery, through an ambulance journey, through accident and emergency (A&E) into emergency surgery to discharge.

An Example of Best Practice in Speed of Treatment

A woman was aware she was having a heart attack on a bus, but she knew the bus would pass her doctor's surgery, so she waited. On reaching her GP practice they called an ambulance which took her to the local hospital, about a 20-minute journey. While in the ambulance she was informed that on arrival at the hospital 'she would be descended upon by many people all with a job to do. Don't worry they know what they are doing'. And so it was, this is exactly what happened and within about an hour she had had two stents fitted and was in recovery, job done. Several years later she has not had any further problems.

The technique that made this possible was to make a process map of the process, analyse it and improve it, as explained later in this chapter.

This was exactly similar to a Formula One pit stop in which four wheels are fitted and the fuel tank refilled in less than 10 seconds. The process had been analysed movement by movement, the best sequence of tasks identified and operatives trained to do only what was needed and in the correct sequence.

In both of these examples, the heart attack and the Formula One pit stop, the planners had identified the critical path, the series of steps that took the longest time to perform, found ways to speed the process up and then introduced the procedure into the everyday work.

Unfortunately, many things can go wrong in this process – delays, mistakes and errors of judgement. Patient's expectations can be unrealistically optimistic, but equally so, many patients can be very modest or humble in their expectations.

Why Create a Process Map?

One of the most powerful methods in any improvement programme is to use process mapping to identify the processes relevant to your work, to analyse the steps in each process and to identify the inputs, the outputs and, from those, the internal customers and suppliers.

After that, unnecessary steps can be removed, stages can be speeded up and causes of errors identified and eliminated.

It is necessary to analyse very carefully

- All of the work steps which are currently carried out
- The information and materials needed to make a start (inputs)
- Where the information and materials come from
- Who carries out each step
- The sequence of steps
- Where each task is carried out
- What is produced (outputs)
- Who uses the output

Finding Out What the Process Is Now

At the start it is vital to 'walk through' the process and write down what actually happens now, not what people think happens or would like to happen. Refinements can show who carries out each task, typical times to complete each task, the departments involved and any other relevant data. It is only when the process is documented in this way that the people involved can debate improvements, explain their ideas to each other and, finally, agree how to proceed in future.

The final document is then an excellent training tool for new staff or transfers.

Styles of Flowchart/Process Map

Many different styles of flowchart have been devised to meet different requirements, for example work study, computer logic, project management, chemical processing – each has its own style. Do not worry about the style you use, providing you explain the symbols and are consistent.

Flowchart/Process Map Symbols

The symbols used here are taken from the British Standard for Total Quality Management BS 7850 Part 2.[1] These are shown in Table 9.1, following.

Table 9.1   Flowchart Process Map Symbols

Symbol	Purpose
⬭	Start or end point
▭	Action
⬭	Document
◇	Decision
⟶	Connecting flow line

How Are These Elements Put Together?

Imagine someone entering data into a computer. The steps are

- Start task.
- Receive data.
- Check data; if faulty, return it to the provider.

- Enter data.
- Check data.
- If error found, correct it.
- Check again.
- Save data.
- Print report.
- End task.

This is a simple process and only involves a single person. It is also a repetitive process, being performed many times an hour.

The process map in Figure 9.4 shows how the internal supplier/customer relationship works. If the data received is not usable, for whatever reason,

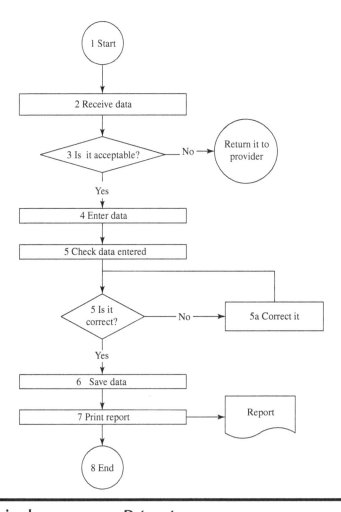

Figure 9.4   A simple process map: Data entry.

then it should be returned to the sender. Only by doing this will the provider get the message that second best is not good enough.

A Further Illustration of a Process Map Example 2

Another example of a process map is shown in Figure 9.5; a car has a puncture and the wheel needs changing. The breakdown is on a main dual carriageway, and you are driving alone. The car has a space-saver spare wheel and all the necessary tools.

Think of all the things you need to do in any order; this is the list I came up with, it is not the correct order:

- Remove wheel.
- Jack car up.
- Remove wheel studs.
- Replace wheel studs.
- Check spare tyre for correct pressure.
- Take all the shopping out of the boot (to get to the spare and tools).
- Park the car safely.
- Put hi-viz jacket on.
- Put warning triangle out.
- Let jack down.
- Get jack out of the boot.
- Get wheel brace out of the boot.
- Put tools back in boot.
- Put dead wheel back in boot.
- Put shopping back in boot.
- Check everything back in car.
- Retrieve triangle and put it in boot.
- Remove hi-viz jacket.
- Get in car and drive off.
- Call for roadside assistance.

Now put these steps into the best sequence and use a flowchart to create a process map. Post-it notes on a board are useful for creating the correct order. In this example, there is a start point, a circle; many tasks, rectangles; some decisions, diamonds; several wait points and an end point, circles. The result drawn in Microsoft Visio is shown in Figure 9.5 (N.B. All process maps have been created in Visio).

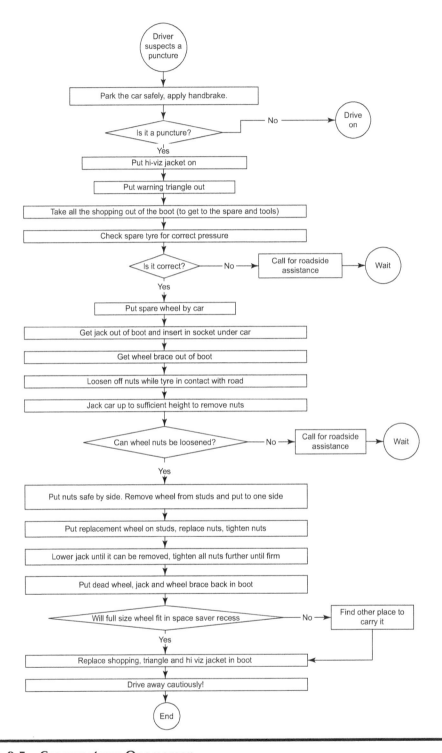

Figure 9.5 Car puncture: One person.

When I was creating this example for the book, the previous list was my first list, but as I put the chart together I realised that some of the wording should be changed and other tasks and decisions were necessary. This is usually the case because the most realistic result is needed.

Note, this for most of us is a very infrequent occurrence, and we would rarely have to use it, but you could keep it as a checklist with the spare wheel (if your car still has one). The puncture process though is very popular with trainers for drawing process maps.

The Process Map with a Helper

Having looked at the puncture repair process for one person I then considered how different it would be if the driver had a passenger, and I rearranged the process map to show how the second person could assist, as shown in Figure 9.6.

This actually happened to me one afternoon when I was returning from a fell walk with three friends in North Wales. We had walked from a car park that was about five miles down a very narrow single-track road with passing places. As we drove home a local car in front of us appeared to be having trouble. It turned out to be a puncture. Because the road was single track with high hedges on both sides, the disabled car was blocking the road. A roadside rescue vehicle would be at least an hour away if we could get a mobile phone signal. The best course of action was to replace the flat tyre.

We were all engineers, technologists and scientists of one sort or other, and within a minute or so we had organised ourselves to change the wheel for the unfortunate elderly lady driver and organise some sort of traffic control.

Within about 10 minutes the lucky lady was on the move, for which she was very grateful.

What we had done was to more or less follow the second process map, Figure 9.6, which applies to a driver with a helper.

Obviously, we did not have a piece of paper to follow, but we all had a very good mental picture of what needed to be done. This is often true in a working environment – the experts have gone through the process so many times that the map is in their heads. But, and this is a big but, when improvements and changes are needed involving a team of workers it is extremely useful to have a large working chart to scribble on! It is a superb communication tool.

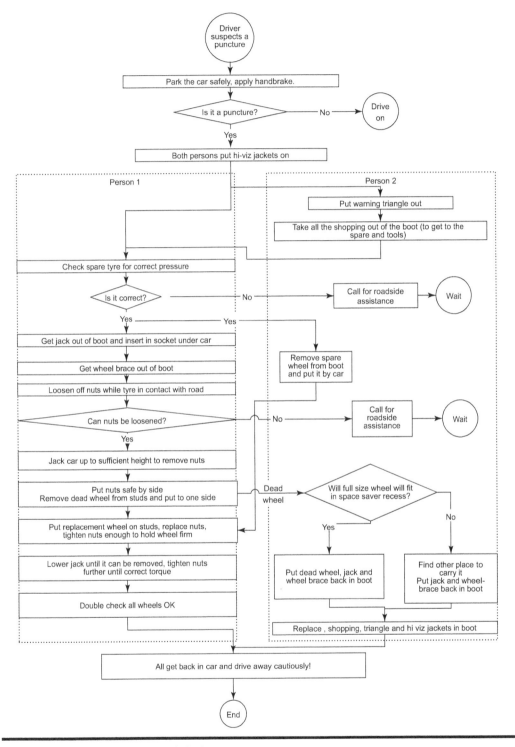

Figure 9.6 Car puncture with helper.

Internal Customers and the Chain of Quality

The Chain of Quality,[2] a term coined by John Groocock, Vice President for Quality at two large US corporations, ITT and TRW, is a series of tasks within a larger process where one department's output(s) are another department's input(s), and so on until there is a final end result that goes to the ultimate customer.

The 'Chain of Quality' concept gives rise to the terms 'internal supplier' and 'internal customer'. The internal customer is like all customers and wants to be 'satisfied' with the input given to them and if dissatisfied should make an internal customer complaint to their internal supplier.

The Blood Sample Example

Figure 9.7, an example of a common healthcare process, shows an illustration of a relatively simple work arrangement, the taking of a blood sample in a diagnostic and treatment process. This particular process map would be very useful should there have been a breakdown in communications between the consultant, the nurse and the laboratory. If it was printed out on A3 paper, several people could sit around it and make suggestions about improvements in their particular departments.

READER WARNING

This process map is only intended as a learning example. It is not intended to be an accurate presentation of actual procedure.

Explanation of the Blood Sample Example

In this example there are 32 process steps. Each step has inputs and outputs, which are the patient's symptoms, verbal instructions, a syringe, blood and written request, laboratory report, consultant's written instruction, correct medication, observations of the patient and the consultant's written conclusion.

Four sub-sections are shown, one each for the patient, the consultant, the nurse and the laboratory, so it is possible to track the work between the departments.

The process maps are for a fictitious process created as an example by the author and do not represent what actually happens at any known

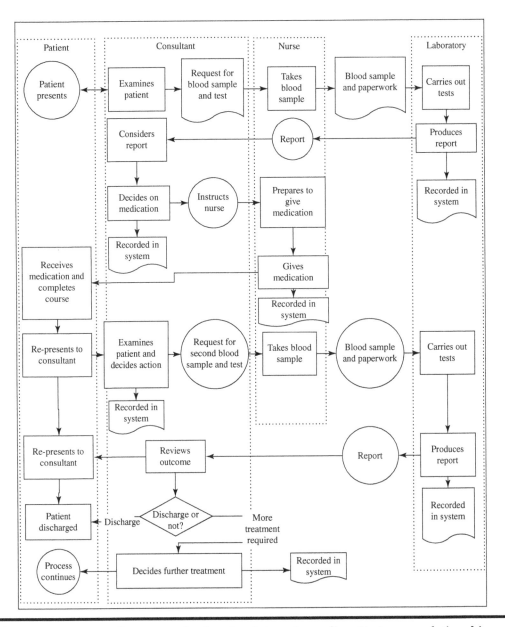

Figure 9.7   Process flow example showing internal supplier: Customer relationships.

hospital. However, reader, when you study it compare it with what happens in your hospital and see if you can improve it.

The chain in the example is

- The consultant's output is a request for tests, which is the input to the nurse.

- The nurse's output is the blood sample and a test request, which is the input to the laboratory.
- The laboratory provides an output, the analysis report, which is the input to the consultant.
- The consultant gives an output, a prescription for medication, which is an input for the nurse.
- The nurse's output is the medication (an input) for the patient.

In this example, the nurse is an internal customer of the consultant and needs to know what tests are required.

The laboratory is an internal customer of the nurse, needing an uncontaminated sample of blood and clear description of the tests required.

The consultant is an internal customer of the laboratory and needs speedy, accurate test results.

The nurse is then an internal customer of the consultant needing clear instructions regarding what medication to give to the patient.

The patient is the customer of everyone.

It is obvious that any fault in this 'chain' will affect the end result, without necessarily being obvious to any of the participants who are the links in the chain.

For many organisations the concept of internal customers and suppliers is difficult to appreciate and a very difficult one to get people to accept, especially when there are large differences in grades and perceived status between participants, for example is a nurse willing and able to tell a consultant that their instructions are consistently unclear and garbled? Is a patient in a strong position to tell the consultant that they are rude and a bully? (I have actually seen and heard it.)

Note, this map is for a process that is repeated many times a day and should 'run like clockwork' or, as an old boss of mine once said, 'shelling peas', if you can remember what that was like.

Queues and Queuing

Unfortunately, in many processes there is a queue, either people in a line, documents in a pile or emails in an inbox.

In the blood sample example, there could be a queue of samples waiting to be tested by the laboratory.

Consider the process of preparing a letter going to a patient's GP. The healthcare professional holds a consultation with the patient and then prepares notes to be typed by a healthcare secretary, who prepares the letter and sends it. At the same time, there are other patients' drafts from that consultant and other consultants giving the secretary drafts to type for all their patients. A pile of work is created for the healthcare secretaries. The letters may finally have to be checked and signed by the consultant. The time to prepare a draft and to type it is often small compared with the time the work sits in a pile. Imagine a situation in which the handwriting is 100% legible and the secretary is 100% accurate – there would be no need for checking. A stage would have been removed from the process.

It is well known that in this queuing situation, where there are piles of work at each workstation, the time for a piece of work to go through the whole process is severely increased by each queue and each piece of work.

If the worker at each workstation was waiting for work, a single piece of work would 'whistle through the pipeline'. This concept has led to the 'just in time' philosophy where the work process is planned so that there is a minimum of waiting time. Every piece of work arrives when it is expected, and there is no work in the queue ahead of it; the total amount of time across the process is only a fraction of what it would have been in the previous way of working.

This example is typical of the type of problem to be solved by a process mapping exercise to provide a method whereby a letter is produced as quickly and accurately as possible. Considering that every department in every hospital has the same process, one wonders why there is not a universal and standard method to be used everywhere, as there is for changing wheels and refuelling a racing car.

One reason why there is not is that every consultant has a different way of producing drafts and the technology available is changing each year, for example audio tapes, emails, text messages and so on.

Critical Paths

Identifying the critical path is the technique used to identify the process path that takes the longest time and is the 'bottleneck' or rate determining path in the process.

The method by which Formula One racing car pit teams can change four wheels and fill the fuel tank in less than 10 seconds has already been discussed.

Do you put the kettle on first at breakfast and do other things while it is boiling? Do you put the turkey in to cook in the oven while you prepare all the other food for Christmas (or Thanksgiving) lunch? When do you roast the potatoes to serve them hot and crisp? These are all small examples about critical path analysis that many people are very familiar with, but do not realise it when working by instinct.

If this analysis is taken one step further and work times are shown for each task, the route that takes the longest time can be identified. For Christmas dinner, preparing and cooking the turkey is often the 'critical path' (it all depends on the menu) and so is started at the appropriate time of the day, with everything else being fitted around it. However, roasting the potatoes and making Yorkshire puddings (a savoury to accompany the main course, not a dessert, called popovers in the United States), often in the same oven, is another job that has to be timed carefully, and a good cook will have a schedule of timings to make sure everything comes together at the right time *and* on time.

Similarly, if you are giving one or more rooms in your house a complete makeover have you worked out the best sequence to do it in? You don't want to paint the walls before you have painted the ceiling, the walls will get splashed and need 'touching up'. For the same reason you don't lay the flooring before you have painted the walls. The flooring could take several weeks to be delivered, so best to order it well in advance, but not too soon you might have to pay for it earlier than you would like to.

A friend of mine who was having her kitchen refitted tried to convince the kitchen fitter that it was not a good idea to allow the very expensive floor covering to be laid before fitting the base cabinets in case the flooring was damaged in the process. It was, and he had to have it replaced at his expense.

All of these examples are about workflow planning, making sure work is done in such a sequence that it is carried out in the shortest time possible without having to repeat anything.

As we discussed earlier, a series of actions that form a work process can be analysed into the component parts and put in the best sequence, also showing who carries out each task.

So it is the same for many jobs in the workplace, and the experienced workers will have their work process mapped out in their heads. But what if steps in the process have been changed and processing times have changed? There will be a need to analyse the new and changed process so that the steps are sequenced correctly *and* as many tasks are carried out simultaneously as possible.

Having identified the first and major bottleneck, methods can be devised for speeding this part of the process up. But then having made those tasks quicker another route will become the new rate determining path, and so on until a point when worthwhile improvements are not economically possible.

Identifying the Critical Paths, Making the Process Faster

Having created a process map, if the problem being addressed is one of making it faster the activities in the process must be looked at in great detail. Your aim as a process improver is to break down all of the activities into their component parts in such a way that if you were to employ as many people as possible to work simultaneously, they could each be working on all the component parts of every activity. The aim is to redraw the process map so there are as many parallel paths of activity, all able to be worked on simultaneously if necessary. The critical path would be the chain of activities 'in series' that takes the longest to complete. The concept of parallel and series activities is shown in Figure 9.8.

A more complex process map will have several chains running simultaneously 'in parallel' alongside each other. That process map will have both series and parallel activities. The process map in Figure 9.5 is a single series of activities because there is only one person to carry them out. Figure 9.6 shows how some activities can be carried out 'in parallel'.

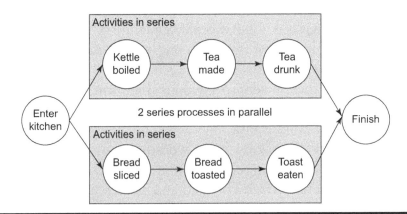

Figure 9.8 Series and parallel activities.

Figure 9.8 shows a simple example of series and parallel activities that might happen at breakfast time. The reader will notice that for this example the author is a drinker of tea (not coffee) made in a pot, and likes to buy unsliced bread.

To have the meal in as short a time as possible you would have the kettle boiling and the toaster toasting in parallel. But you can't eat the bread until it is toasted; slicing the bread, toasting and eating must be in series.

Also notice that in each activity box the description of the action is the completion of the task described, for example 'kettle boiled'.

So is there a critical path? That depends on how long each activity takes, and in this example the timescales are very short, but at a guess it will take longer for the kettle to boil and the tea to brew (the experts say it takes 5 minutes for the flavour to develop) making the tea-making the critical path if the bread toasts in less time than the tea brews.

Gantt Charts

A Gantt chart is a simpler form of project planning aid. Named after Henry Gantt who developed the technique in the 1910s, it consists of a column of tasks on the left with a row showing the timeline for each row/task. The columns represent days, weeks or months depending on the project. Each task is represented by a bar in the row. Responsibilities can be shown against each task. Table 9.2 is an example of a typical chart in which the shaded boxes show when the activities are planned to happen.

Some Tips for Preparing Gantt Charts

1. Brainstorm every activity/task that is needed to carry out the project.
2. On the brainstorming list work out a rough sequence. If some items are trivial, group them with other tasks appropriately.
3. Transfer the list to the process map/Gantt chart in sequence downwards.
4. Estimate a timescale across the columns with each column representing a day, week or month.
5. Enter the bars on the chart showing when each task starts and finishes.

Table 9.2 Example Gantt Chart

Task	Resp. of	Involving	Week 1	Week 2	Week 3	Week 4	Week 5	Week 6	Etc. →
					Project Plan				
Planning meeting	JB	Team	X						
Gather data	MS	Team	X	-------	X				
Etc.									

6. Draw a straight line between the ends of any tasks that must be done in sequence.
7. Calculate when the project will be completed according to this first plan.
8. Now mark on each bar who will be doing the job and an estimate of the time needed in hours or days.
9. Calculate how much time each person needs within each column to do the task and create a histogram as in the example.
10. Experiment by moving tasks around to see if the job can be done in less time.
11. Sign and date your final plans.

Planning to Decorate a Room Using a Gantt Chart

Moving to a more complex example than eating breakfast, consider decorating a room using a Gantt chart to find the critical path. This example is a one-off, unique project compared with a repetitive process which is carried out day after day, and decorating is a good way to explain critical paths.

You have bought an old house which needs renovation. You and your partner want the bedroom gutted and completely redecorated. You are going to prepare a process map to plan, after you have gutted the room, the rewiring and the selection and delivery of carpets, curtains, light fittings, wallpaper, paint, furniture and bedding.

So what do you know about the timescales involved? First allow time for shopping, say 5 days. Availability of the items you need is

Carpets: 6 weeks
Curtains: 4 weeks, and 2 days warning for the curtain fitter
Light fittings: Off the shelf
Wallpaper, paint: Off the shelf
New bed and furniture: 5 weeks
Bedding: Off the shelf
Rewiring: 1 day

You are working 12-hour shifts and work in a bar on your days off, so you must employ a decorator and an electrician. In his quotation the electrician says he can complete the rewiring in 1 day and needs 2 weeks advance notice. The decorator says he can complete the room in 3 days, but needs 3 weeks advance notice before he can start. What is the quickest time (the critical path) to complete the room fully and spend a night in it? How could this be reduced?

A quick overview suggests that the furniture on 5 weeks delivery is one of the time limiting steps and should be ordered very early, if not first.

It is also obvious that the decorator cannot start until the room is rewired, so he must move in immediately after the electrician has finished.

The carpets cannot be laid until the decorator has finished, and the furniture cannot be put in place until the carpets are down.

At first glance then it looks as though the main sequence is

Rewire, decorate, lay carpets, hang curtains, receive and fit the furniture, make the bed and sleep there.

One further factor – you need 5 days off work to choose all the décor and inform the workmen when they will be required. You can have this time off from Saturday 7 May until Thursday 12 May. You also need to know when you need to take flexi-time off to check the work.

So what is the process map going to look like? It is shown in Figure 9.9, but this time it is different from the process maps shown earlier because, being a unique one-off project, the timing can be shown on a Gantt chart. In this figure the timescale columns have been omitted.

From this chart you calculate that the delivery of carpets is on the critical path, and any delay there would hold up moving into the bedroom. The carpets would be fitted 47 days after starting, and you could move the bed in on the 48th day, 24 June.

If the curtains were to be delivered within (28 + 5) 33 days, they could be fitted as soon as the decorator is finished.

The electrician and decorator have 23 days slack time. Slack time is the difference between the time they need for the job and the time length of the critical path. That means they have flexibility in the dates available to them before the electrician has to start.

Obviously, if the carpet supplier rang to say that because of a cancelled order the carpet could be delivered in 21 days, the whole map would change and would be recalculated.

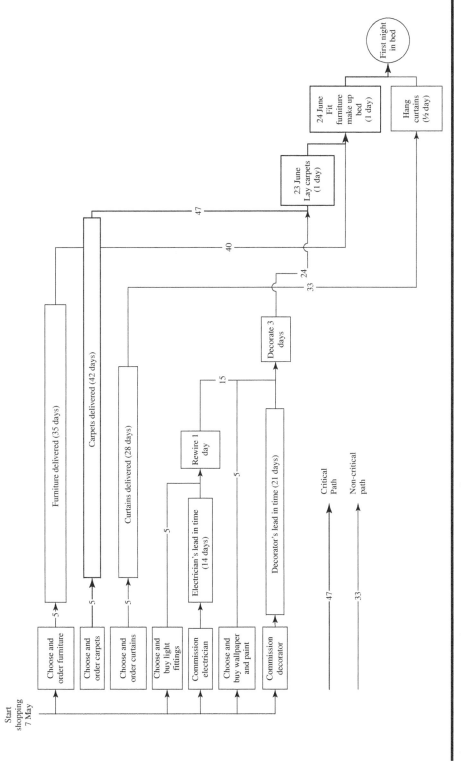

Figure 9.9   Decorating process map/Gantt chart.

In Brief

To summarise, each patient goes through a process with personal expectations of the process. If these expectations are not achieved the process (or service) will be deemed by the patient to have failed; the aim of the NHS is to influence patients to have realistic expectations and for these expectations to be met at every stage, every time for every patient.

To achieve this, every employee must be capable of doing his or her job successfully and courteously; the equipment must be up to date and work to specification every time and all of the time.

If equipment does not work or when a mistake is made, steps must be taken to prevent that incident from happening again. Everyone must 'buy into' or 'subscribe to' this philosophy.

The message from this section is that process mapping is a powerful tool to help people carry out their work as quickly and as effectively as is known at that time, and the process map shows everyone how the job is done, and if they do not agree they can make a better version and try to sell it to the others in the team.

Chapter 10

Continuous Improvement Processes

SUMMARY

Each of the processes for improving quality is put into perspective. Three processes are discussed:

- The continuous improvement process
- The problem-solving process (Chapter 13)
- The innovation process

Three Quality Improvement Processes

These three processes are explained below, signposting the reader to subsequent chapters.

1. The Continuous Improvement Process

Having discussed the work processes in Chapter 9, the next type of process to discuss is the continuous improvement process that has the following four steps:

Step A: Monitor the current performance against existing standards.
Step B: Eliminate causes of poor performance with the problem-solving process.

Step C: Raise the standards against which performance is measured.
Step D: Monitor performance against the new (better) standard. Go back
      to Step B.

This is like the training of an athlete. The existing standard is the athlete's current personal best (PB) performance. The causes of poor performance could be injury, lack of stamina or poor diet. More training is used to set a new PB (the raised standard). All subsequent performances are compared against the new PB. Further training is used to increase the PB further, with a series of marginal gains.

Many standards refer to this approach as PDCA, plan-do-check-act, and the ways to start this process are described in Chapter 11.

2. **The Problem-Solving Process**

The second process of the three, problem solving, is Step B in the previous list showing the continuous improvement process, and this is explained in Chapter 13, the main topic of this book.

3. **The Innovation Process: Proactive Improvements**

There is another dimension to improvement, and that is the proactive innovation process. So far we have discussed 'error elimination', reacting to the negative. It is equally important to look at a process and say 'we can do it better than this' or 'can we not find a better way to … arrange appointments … heal a wound … repair a knee … restore sight, and so on?'

Innovation does not have to be ground-breaking new technology such as using stem cells to repair body parts. It can be as simple as relocating a workstation to speed up an activity.

The sum total of all ideas for innovation can be summarised in Figure 10.1. In Britain, ideas can come from

- Patients
- Healthcare workers with internal experiences and ideas
- Major incidents
- Professional investigations and reports
- Government, the National Health Service (NHS) directorate, health trusts, clinical commissioning groups (CCG)

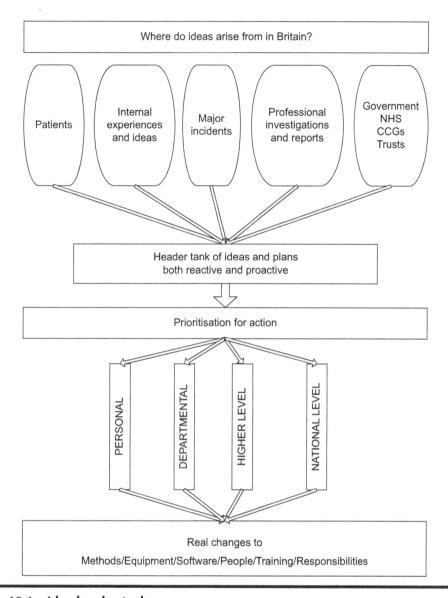

Figure 10.1 Idea header tank.

Some will arise after an incident, and that is called being 'reactive'; others will be proposed as ideas to prevent undesirable incidents before they happen, say following a risk analysis, and this is being 'proactive'.

It should be self-evident that taking proactive action is preferred, because this is taking preventive action before adverse results can happen, just like the old adage 'a stitch in time saves nine'.

Schematic Representation of Where Ideas Can Come From

In Figure 10.1 the diagram shows the five sources just listed where ideas can come from. These would be put on an overall register. Some people call this register a 'header tank'. By mutual agreement these ideas would be prioritised for importance and ease of implementation as described in Chapter 21. When they are acted upon it would mean that real changes would be made in methods, equipment, software and people's level of training and responsibility. Any such changes would be documented and could be audited by external inspectors looking for an audit trail of evidence of improvement processes taking place.

Some organisations attempt to do too much too quickly, and they achieve nothing; better to choose carefully and succeed than appear to be busy. A general manager once said, 'Let us decide now what improvements you are *not* going to work on'.

Learning from Experience

When work does not go as planned, or when there is a complaint, various words are used to describe the adverse event such as error, mistake, variation, opportunity, concern, complaint, non-conformance and so on. I had a reason to make a complaint to a branch of a well-known chain of opticians recently and was pleased when the manager produced a pre-printed pad on which to record the matter. I was quite amused though to see that it was called 'A Concern' in the heading. The company obviously did not like the word 'complaint', 'concern' was less threatening.

A culture has seemed to have developed in Britain where businesses have started using a spectrum of terms for receiving feedback from customers. It is, in increasing seriousness 1 to 5,

1. A 'Wow' (looking for praise)
2. Feedback (can be positive or negative)
3. Concern (that's starting to look serious)
4. Verbal complaint (this one can be ignored, hopefully; it's not in writing)
5. Written complaint (it's in writing, so we had better do something)
6. Solicitor's letter of intention to sue

The NHS is now using the 'Family and Friends Test' to provide feedback about the healthcare that patients and carers have received, which sits at number 2 in the previous list.

This spectrum of terminology further describes the spectrum of instances of poor care shown in Figure 8.1 in Chapter 8, starting at annoyances, going through rudeness and shoddy care to extreme malpractice. Whatever view is taken, items 3 to 6 all indicate a dissatisfied patient or customer, and regardless of the word or words your workplace might use to describe something that does not go correctly, it is most important that there are the right processes to deal with any negative situation and whether they treat that situation with sufficient gravity.

When the mistake/error/variation means failure to meet a patient's expectations or to produce a positive outcome, most people expect any healthcare service to 'learn from its mistakes'. This popular saying which uses the word 'mistake' lends credibility to the use of the word 'mistake' to describe adverse events, and so it will be used here.

How does such a complex organisation as the NHS 'learn from its mistakes'? Professor Timothy W. R. Briggs has done just that in his specialist field of orthopaedic surgery. In his 2012 report 'Getting it Right First Time',[1] he provides a comprehensive analysis of the 'variations' in the current outcomes of orthopaedic surgery and shows those with the best results. This is a form of benchmarking. Benchmarking is where the people who are best at a way of working are studied by those who want to improve, and the better methods are adopted by the weaker group. It can also involve comparing the quantitative results obtained and using this comparison to monitor performance.

Learning from mistakes has therefore to happen on a number of different levels, shown in the following Table 10.1.

Negatives and Positives

For those readers who always like to take a positive view of work, all of these comments are about looking at the negative aspects, but this is essential if these negatives are to be identified and eliminated. It is not negative to realise there is a problem, to analyse the root causes of errors and ask how to stop them in future – it is strong leadership.

Table 10.1 Mistakes and Benchmarking

	Level of Mistake	*Action to Benchmark*
Level 1	Personal mistakes	Compare with other people performing well in same job.
Level 2	Departmental mistakes	Compare with similar departments that perform the tasks well.
Level 3	Organisational mistakes (hospitals, clinics, surgeries)	Compare with better performing organisations (hospitals, clinics, surgeries).
Level 4	National mistakes	Compare with internationally renowned organisations.

Over the years I have met many people who do not accept that mistakes should be discussed, it is negative thinking. But as Matthew Syed discusses in his book *Black Box Thinking*, it is only when mistakes are analysed that actions can be taken to stop them happening again.

Chapter 11

Getting Started: Where Are You Now?

SUMMARY

This chapter sets out a checklist for assessing whether there are any opportunities in the reader's organisation for embarking upon a continuous improvement programme.

As you read this you could be in one or a combination of the following situations.

Your workplace in a healthcare organisation, large or small, has been inspected by external inspectors and has received an adverse report stating that improvements must be made. The report will state what the non-compliances are, and a clear documented action plan will be required with deadlines and responsibilities. In this case the methods in this guide can be followed, and most important of all the records described for problem solving will provide your organisation with an audit trail, that is documented evidence of what changes have been made.

Hopefully you won't be in that situation, and the following will be more appropriate.

No one in your place of work has ever considered starting a continuous improvement programme. Work is task driven (i.e. the methods are in place, and everyone gets on with their job without considering whether things could be better or not). There are no measures of performance, and everyone assumes they are doing a good job.

Or, you work in a team of anything from 5 to 50 people led by a supervisor or a manager, and this team may be just one among several with a more senior manager or director responsible for them all. Being a progressive sort of person, you want to see if improvements can be made in your team, but unsurprisingly you do not know where to start.

Or, perhaps you have been appointed to a new supervisory post, a continuous improvement programme has been started and your organisation is faced with a long list of bright ideas for improvement.

Making a Start

By considering the following four questions you could make a report summarising the current position, proposing small but important projects that will make the department more effective. These questions are

> Question 1: Is any monitoring of workplace quality already being carried out?
> Question 2: Is your workplace well organised? Does it function smoothly?
> Question 3: What do you (and your colleagues) think you could do better?
> Question 4: Does everyone in your workplace understand the basic principles for achieving high quality levels?

Take these questions in turn.

Q1: Is Any Monitoring of Workplace Quality Already Being Carried Out?

This could be infection control, waiting times or bed sore incidence, shown as a chart against days, weeks or months or years.

Are these charts up to date? Do they show any trends? Are they linked to an action programme to make improvements? Does anyone take any notice of them?

If the answer to these questions is 'Yes', then your team is doing very well, and most people will have a good understanding of continuous improvement. If not, there is obviously work to do.

Q2: Is Your Workplace Well Organised?
Does It Function Smoothly?

To be well run, a workplace should be organised on the basis of the processes it has to perform.

In this case it is necessary to answer a question with more questions.

- Have the processes that your team carries out been clearly defined?
- Do you know clearly what the inputs are and where they come from, and can you tell whether they are correct and without error?
- If an input is faulty, would you recognise it and know who to approach to correct it?*
- Does everyone know what their job is, and have they been trained to carry it out?
- Is there sufficient cover for unexpected absence, and is that cover trained for the job?
- Does all the equipment work with complete reliability?
- Are your priorities clearly stated, and would you know what to do if there was a clash of priorities?
- Is your workplace a team or a collection of uncoordinated individuals?
- Is your manager a leader or a controller?
- Whatever your team's outputs are, can you determine whether they are correct, on time and to your customer's satisfaction?
- Is this quality being measured, monitored and reported?

---

* Regarding the asterisk item about faulty inputs, I once came across a workstation where for no apparent reason the electronic components started to fail the quality checks. This continued for a week, and then normal good quality was restored. After extensive checking, it was discovered that the bought-in component for the work had for many months been faulty, but the regular operator, thinking they were doing the department 'a good turn', had been making a small modification to correct each item. When that operator went on holiday and a deputy stood in, that person did not know that a correction had to be made and the item was passed on, only to be rejected at a later stage. The failure here was that the faulty items should have been reported back to the original supplier, but it wasn't through ignorance and inaction. There should always be the means to report sub-standard work, otherwise the organisation does not learn.

This anecdote also illustrates another principle; Charles Vincent in *Patient Safety*[1] reported that

> *The very ingenuity and resourcefulness that are rightly admired in clinical staff, and that produce immediate benefits for patients, can inhibit more fundamental organisational change.*

Vincent quotes researchers Tucker and Edmundson, who found a nurse who said

> *Working around problems is just part of my job. By being able to get i.v. (intravenous) bags or whatever else I need, it enables me to do my job and to have a positive impact on a person's life.*

The researchers commented,

> *Although admirable and reminiscent of the qualities espoused in high-reliability organisations, this resourcefulness can mean nothing ever changes, as no one is informed that there were no i.v. bags there when there should have been.*
> *This is effective in the short term but prevents problems from surfacing as an opportunity or improvement.*

In the language of this book, 'Lessons are not (being) learned'.

Q3: What Do You (and Your Colleagues) Think You Could Do Better?

Thinking of your department, do you know of examples that would answer any of the following questions in Table 11.1?

The list in Table 11.1 covers most of the types of improvement that would form the basis of a continuous improvement programme, and it can be used as a checklist for making a start. The items on the list are not mutually exclusive, for example a customer complaint may be that something is not happening fast enough.

Table 11.1   Ideas for Doing Better

- Is something happening regularly which is undesirable?
- Do all the inputs to the department meet the required standard and on time?
- Do some jobs take longer than you think they should?
- Do some jobs take longer than the boss thinks they should?
- Do some jobs take longer than our customers/patients think they should?
- Does any work need correcting before it goes out?
- Does any work 'come back' from the recipient, because it was not correct 'first time'?
- Do you get complaints from internal customers?
- Do you get complaints from patients/external customers?
- Is there a less costly way of working without affecting the standard of work?

Q4 Does Everyone in Your Workplace Understand the Basic Principles for Achieving High Quality Levels?

In this context, 'high quality levels' means completing work correctly, on time, every time, to the complete satisfaction of the recipient, whether that recipient is a patient, a customer or a colleague in another department or organisation, with a smile.

Your Workplace

What are the processes of the teams in your workplace? When you receive information or materials from other departments or teams, are they always correct and on time? Are there weak links in the internal chain, and are your team outputs always correct and on time? You need to ask your customers to find out.

The Appointments Example

An appointments clerk/receptionist has an empty diary or diaries and a list of patients for one or more specialists at the start a session for booking appointments (the input). When the work is complete there will be diary entries and associated appointment notifications for the patients (the outputs), and this is the finish of the appointment-making process.

In a perfect world that would be the end of the process; everyone, both patients and professionals, would turn up on time and it would be 100% successful. Unfortunately, events will occur, and not everyone will turn up on time (or turn up at all), and the subsequent processes will not be 100% efficient. But that is another problem.

Let us apply some quality principles to the appointments diary example here. At first glance the specialist for whom the appointment is being made would appear to be the internal customer and the appointments clerk the supplier. Suppose, however, that the specialist failed to tell the appointments clerk that there was a time when he/she would not be available. An appointment would be made for that time, the patient would turn up, the specialist would not be there and there would be wasted time. The patient is not impressed (a dissatisfied external customer).

Applying the internal supplier–customer relationship to this example, the specialist is the supplier of open diary appointment times and the clerk is the customer. By omitting to advise the clerk of a change to the available times, the specialist has supplied poor-quality information or an incorrect input. Like all incorrect or faulty inputs, problems then occur further down the process.

To achieve high quality levels, whatever it is that you do, whatever your outputs are they must arrive on time, correct and acceptable to your customer, whether internal or external. From an economical point of view the outputs must also be within agreed cost limits.

In summary, high levels of quality will be provided when the agreed outputs from your department are

- Correct to agreed standards,
- On time,
- Within agreed costs,
- And with a smile!

Yes, that final point is important!

Idea-Generating Meetings

When groups of workers are asked to volunteer possible ideas for improvement in their workplace, they usually come up with very vague ideas such as

- Poor communications
- Poor attitudes
- Technical faults
- Low output
- Lack of time

Problems raised during these sessions are much more subjective or vague than the previous list, and pose the problem solver a much more difficult task. Each idea should be queried strongly to determine exactly what the proposer has in mind. Such broad ideas are best challenged with 'Why is that a problem?' (see the Five Whys in Chapter 15).

By asking 'Why?' again and again, eventually you will reach a hint of what the core problem is, but at this stage it might only be a hint. As in many murder investigations, a lot more footwork may need to be done before the core problem can be clearly identified.

During these discussions people often talk in generalities, it is easier than having to think about specifics. This tendency is discussed in S. J. Hayakawa and Alan R. Hayakawa's book *Language in Thought and Action*.[2] They in turn refer to a concept called the Abstraction Ladder originated by Alfred Korzybski in *Science and Sanity*[3] (Figure 11.1).

To understand the Abstraction Ladder, think of two types of personalities – practical people who 'have their feet on the ground' and not so practical people who have their 'head in the clouds'.

Think of the top of the Abstraction Ladder as being in the clouds. The words there are very broad and general. Knowing what these words mean is difficult because they are imprecise.

The base of the ladder is on the ground; words there are very specific and precise. Words at levels in between the base and the clouds are increasingly less precise as we move up to the top.

The learning point is that, whenever you are interviewing, if vague abstract words are used, question the speaker until you can determine precisely what they are talking about.

Imagine you are interviewing someone to find out why queues keep building up at a reception desk. They tell you that the equipment is always breaking down. The word equipment is at the top of the Abstraction Ladder, and to understand the situation you need to come down to a more precise term. Further questioning leads to the answer that the appointments letters will not print out on printer 3. 'Will not print out' is less vague but still imprecise.

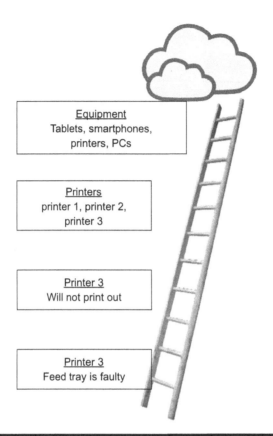

Figure 11.1 The Abstraction Ladder.

On more questioning, it appears that there is one specific printer that is unreliable and the fault is a paper feed tray. So through persistent questioning, 'equipment' turns out to be the feed tray on a specific printer. This is a very simple example but enough, I hope, to explain the principle.

This technique is also valuable during audits, which can often fail because they do not get to a sufficient level of detail and as that old adage goes, 'The Devil is in the detail'.

Before getting started on your first project it is important to consider the implications of embarking on a continuous improvement programme. These implications are that unless each problem-solving exercise is closely managed there is a chance of failure, and for the problem to be eliminated you must all be prepared to make effective changes to make the difference, otherwise the 'status quo' will continue. Any changes made must be permanent and become part of the way of working.

Having researched these four questions you should have a list of possible projects. For you and your team to learn how to progress these projects, choose a simple one and put it through the stages in Chapter 13 onwards. Consider this possible project and summarise your thinking by agreeing with your colleagues a project objective filling in the unknowns in the following statement:

> '**We would like to examine** (*a process, e.g. booking appointments*) **because** (*the problem, e.g. patients complain they have to wait too long*) **and if we could make improvements we could** (*the benefit, e.g. ensure everyone is seen when they need to be*)'.

Keep your summary as simple as that! It is the first stage of defining the core problem. Later we will discuss creating a problem record sheet, this simple previous statement feeds into the problem-solving process and helps everyone think about it and understand the nature of the problem.

Things to Consider before Starting

If any continuous improvement project is going to make real change then at least one of the following in Table 11.2 must happen when the recommendations are implemented.

Table 11.2   Changes that Must Occur

- People must be given more training, be redeployed or made redundant; and/or
- Changes must be made to the business process to make more information available more quickly; and/or
- Methods must be changed; and/or
- Work locations must be changed; and/or
- Responsibilities must change; and/or
- New equipment must be bought; and/or
- New software and/or hardware must be bought; and/or
- Existing equipment must be repaired effectively; and/or
- Existing software must be modified.

Cost

Most continuous improvement projects, whether large or small, will during their development and implementation stages have an immediate cost affecting the financial performance of the unit. This will be either in people's time taken to develop new methods or in the cost of new equipment/materials. This cost must be controlled by constant monitoring and review, proportionate to the size of the project.

Overall Control, the Need to Manage Multiple Continuous Improvement Projects

It is often the case that not even the chief executive knows how many projects are being worked on, what they are costing, where they are up to and what ultimate impact they would have on the business. To be effective the whole programme must be managed and lead by senior people. To that end, Chapter 22 shows how this can be done.

Because of quite normal, but slack, business attitudes and behaviours, the success rate of ad hoc methods when introducing change in business can be very low. Very few organisations have the ability to run major continuous

Table 11.3 Why Projects Fail

> - The reasons for making change were inadequately defined.
> - The aims were unclear or ambiguous.
> - Insufficient time was allowed for the development work.
> - Other work pressures took priority.
> - The project did not have a sufficiently powerful sponsor. (The sponsor is a senior person, e.g. a director, who can if necessary force through the changes needed.)
> - The data available to appraise the current situation was inadequate.
> - Team members were not sufficiently skilled to understand the current situation or devise better methods.
> - The problem spanned several departments, some of which did not participate.
> - Project creep took over, sometimes called 'moving the goalposts'.
> - Management was in too big a hurry to get results.
> - Insufficient capital was available to overcome root causes.
> - Personal politics put ring fences around existing, but inadequate, methods (sacred cows).

improvement projects effectively without trained help. The most common reasons why continuous improvement projects have failed are presented in Table 11.3.

These reasons should make it clear to the reader that a fully coordinated programme is needed across all departments of the organisation, based on the organisation's operational processes, impacting on measurable targets and made the responsibility of a very senior management team.

What Next?

So what happens next? Where should we start? How do we start?

In Chapter 13 we will consider a process for resolving problems. This process has been tried and tested in many situations and brings a structured approach to what can often be a stressful and chaotic time for the participants, especially when there are high stakes such as large financial losses or danger to patients.

By following a publicised process the aims, steps, priorities and methods can be clearly communicated to all concerned. This avoids the most dangerous action which is to grab at the first idea that is shouted out, probably by one of the bullies in the department. Expensive changes are then made, all to no avail. I use strong language here because I have seen it happen.

Chapter 12

Quality Improvement in Primary Care

SUMMARY

Small providers of primary care have different needs to those of larger units such as hospitals when implementing quality improvement. The actions or inaction of the owner or senior partner/director can make or break any attempt at improvement.

The way quality improvement can be applied in healthcare is dependent upon the size and type of the unit providing the service. In Britain, on the one hand there are the very large hospital trusts employing hundreds and financed centrally, providing 'secondary and tertiary care'. On the other hand, there are smaller units employing dozens, providing 'primary care', of which many are run as small independent businesses funded by the National Health Service (NHS). There are then the care homes that interface with the NHS that are run by local councils and independent providers.

Although these providers receive income from the NHS, or in the case of care homes from the local council, they must make a financial surplus each year to be able to invest in new and better equipment and premises. They work to a different financial model and consequently have different priorities and styles of management.

On its website, NHS England[1] describes primary care as

- Eye health
- Dental
- Medical
- Pharmacy

Each of these types of service provider is generally perceived by the public as giving the community service on behalf of the NHS. However, many of these are either private or public limited companies, run by their own management team, delivering services under contract and inspected by the Care Quality Commission (CQC).

This chapter is about the problems of applying quality improvement in smaller privately run healthcare providers.

So what is a small business? In some professional practices, law for example, it is considered that if there are no more than three senior professionals each can operate relatively independently, but with four or more a managing partner is required. The spectrum of size spans therefore from a sole practitioner through a 4- or 5-partner practice to a 10- or 20-partner business and beyond.

The quality or professionalism of small businesses is very much down to the strength of personality and level of personal professional standards of the lead partner.

In Table 12.1 the 2×2 matrix suggests the result of having the combinations of strong or weak leaders with high or low professional standards. With a weak leader with low standards (Box 1) the practice goes nowhere. For a strong leader with high standards (Box 4), excellence is achievable. A strong leader with low standards (Box 2) leads everyone to disaster, and a weak leader with high standards (Box 3) will just get everyone frustrated, themselves especially.

Anyone who works in a small practice might be able to recognise where in this matrix the practice leader sits. To make improvements the practice as a whole needs to move upwards and to the right of the matrix, and this can only be done if all of those involved understand the position and are prepared, with teamwork, to help each other to change.

Thus, on one hand, for the senior partner with low standards (Boxes 1 and 2), if he/she accepts the need to improve, he/she can be mentored by a trusted senior person and hopefully move to Box 3 or 4. But one wonders

Table 12.1 Outcomes for a Practice according to the Personal Characteristics of the Senior Partner/Owner

	Low Personal Professional Standards ↓	*High Personal Professional Standards* ↓
STRONG LEADER →	Box 2 Leads everyone to disaster	Box 4 Achieves excellence
WEAK LEADER →	Box 1 Practice goes nowhere	Box 3 Frustration all round

how the person got in the senior position in the first place, they would probably be the owner. The weak leader on the other hand (Box 1 or 3) needs a strong team around themselves if the practice is going to achieve higher standards.

Table 12.1 obviously does not only apply to healthcare but to any profession.

The issues faced by small practices are those faced by any small business; principally, the lack of reserve people to provide cover when a member of staff is off sick or when there is an epidemic and secondly, cash flow for new equipment and maintenance.

The best practices will have a very capable senior partner and a strong administrator who can run a 'tight ship'. Often this partner will have the skill of selecting and motivating the best people, especially ones who are caring and compassionate. The partners will be good listeners who can act accordingly on what they hear and will be comfortable with change, having the confidence to delegate appropriately.

The best practices will ensure that all employees are fully trained, not only in their specialism, but in customer care and dealing with people.

Delegation

Successful delegation is vitally important in the small practice, it gives the senior partner more time to plan, mentor and direct. Here in Table 12.2 is another 2×2 matrix to help anyone to delegate. Delegation is a matter of trust. Can the person be trusted to do the job efficiently and in a timely manner? Does the person know his/her limits enough to stop and ask for advice; and if they do so will the delegator be prepared to stop, listen and advise?

Person type 1 in the matrix with low skills and low motivation is a passenger, and no business can support passengers. They are probably in the wrong job – help them to find their preferred job, elsewhere.

Person type 2 is very capable but needs motivating, they will do the job well but slowly. Do not give them urgent work, nor long-term work, they will never finish it.

Person type 3 has potential if they have the ability to learn, but they may use their initiative too much and overstep their capability; have frequent and regular supervisory sessions with them to develop their skill set.

Person type 4 is obviously someone who should not be lost to the practice. They should be encouraged, trusted and, if possible, used to mentor others.

Where in this matrix would you put the various people in your workplace?

Table 12.2 How to Regard Individuals When Delegating

		Individual's Motivation	
		Low ↓	High ↓
Relative Skill for Job to Be Done	High →	2 Push the person (can do good work)	4 Trust and encourage (must be retained in the business)
	Low →	1 Passenger (not required)	3 Coach this person (has potential)

Quality Assurance, Quality Control and Improvement

The standards and culture of a small healthcare unit are determined by the personalities of the owner(s) or senior professionals. They need to be visionary and inspirational.

The basic requirements for sound quality assurance in any organisation are to recruit qualified staff with the relevant personal skills, having thoroughly checked their credentials. Also, it is necessary to have a practice procedures manual explaining how the administration of the practice is carried out. This will include how patients will be booked in and how appointments are prioritised and allocated to the relevant professional. There should be procedures for referring patients on to other professionals and how those outcomes are recorded and communicated. Procedures should be in place for ordering (healthcare) consumable materials of the correct specification and how these are checked on receipt, where they are stored and how stocks are monitored. If incorrect or faulty materials have been supplied, instructions should be available for how they are returned to the supplier. Similarly, there should be procedures for the routine maintenance of equipment by qualified persons.

There must be clear procedures for handling complaints and, in the case of personal injury, who in the practice must be involved.

As far as the computer systems are concerned, procedures should explain how records are kept confidential, how the system is backed up, what the disaster recovery plan is and so on.

The Role of the Senior Partner/Owner/Professional

The senior partner must decide how the quality of the work in the practice will be controlled. This is a very delicate matter both for patients and for professionals and beyond the scope of this book. However, there is no substitute for peer review. I had an example where in a professional practice with six professional fee earners the standard for quality assurance ISO 9001 was being installed. In that standard, the organisation must state how the quality of the work is assessed. The senior partner agreed that it would be a good idea for him to audit samples of the other partners' work. In the case of one partner he found that dozens of his colleague's case files had not been closed out when the work had finished. This meant that the financial status was varied, with fees not charged when they should have been. The partner was asked to leave. This would not have been discovered without a rigorous system of peer review.

The senior partner/owner is effectively the only person who can lead an improvement campaign because he/she sets the whole tone and culture of the business. Ultimately, he/she can make or break any move to improve standards. His or her personal work has to be impeccable because there cannot be two sets of standards, one for the owner and another for everyone else. Any bad decision taken by the lead partner can destroy months of hard work to set standards at a higher level.

The Smallest Practices

In the smallest practices, there will not be 'an information technology department', 'a human resources department' or a 'maintenance department', and the employees have to understand this and manage accordingly. It can be especially difficult for those who have previously worked in a large organisation, and it may take time for them to adjust.

Chapter 13

Putting Right What Has Gone Wrong: The Problem-Solving Process

SUMMARY

Using a strict method: A six-step process is shown for making sure that problems are resolved in a structured and disciplined manner.

Introduction to Problem Solving

The expression 'problem solving' can mean many things. Wouldn't it be nice to have a universal formula for solving all our problems at home and at work? Unfortunately, no one has devised the perfect problem-solving method, and so we have to have an individual approach to each different type of problem.

There are, however, some basic principles which can be applied to most workplace situations, and these are presented in this manual.

'Houston, We Have a Problem'

'Houston, we have a problem' is a famous quote from the Apollo 13 mission and has gone into the popular vernacular. What should you do when a colleague says 'We have a problem'?

Two well-known characters, one real, the other fictitious, managed to solve specific problems in a characteristic way.

Alexander the Great and the Gordian Knot

In around 333 BC, in Greek legend, Gordius, King of Gordium in Phrygia, tied a huge intricate knot, and an oracle (a divine prophet) stated that whoever could unravel it would rule Asia. Alexander, later known as Alexander the Great, came along and, instead of trying to disentangle it, took out his sword and cut it in half. He later became ruler of Macedonia, Persia, Egypt and India, at the time the centre of the most advanced civilisations on earth.

Indiana Jones

Most people will remember the scene in the Indiana Jones movie when he had been in numerous hand-to-hand fights and was confronted by a massive tribesman waving a fearsome sword. Everyone expected another hair-raising scrap with swords or knives, but instead Harrison Ford (a.k.a. Indiana Jones) simply took out a gun and shot the man dead. The humour lay in the unexpected way he tackled the problem.

Just because it is customary to approach the situation in a certain way, you don't have to do it that way. If there is a simple way out – take it.

Problems That Do Not Have an Obvious Answer: Structured Problem Solving with a Standard Process

Most real-life problems, however, are not always so easy to solve and have to be tackled in a methodical way. This is called 'the problem-solving process'. There are a number of distinct steps in the classic problem-solving process, and these inevitably vary according to the training course leader. For the purpose of this book there are six steps. This process is shown in Table 13.1, and each is explained in the following chapters.

Table 13.1   The Six Steps for Problem Solving

Step 1 (Chapter 14)	Recognising that one or more problems exist and researching and selecting the one to resolve.
	↓
Step 2 (Chapter 15)	Understanding and defining exactly what the problem is.
	↓
Step 3 (Chapter 16)	Researching and identifying the root causes of that problem.
	↓
Step 4 (Chapter 17)	Removing the root causes – applying 'the solution'.
	↓
Step 5 (Chapter 18)	Proving that a permanent solution has been applied.
	↓
Step 6 (Chapter 19)	Celebrating success, closing the project.

Why Use a Process?

As stated earlier, only a few problems can be solved the way Alexander the Great cut the Gordian knot. Most of the time, the most effective way to solve problems is to use a disciplined method and not to guess or jump to testing the most popular ideas at the time.

I mentioned earlier 'Mr Flapping Coat Tails', the departmental trouble-shooter who was called in to solve printed circuit board processing problems. He always knew exactly what to do because he had seen most problems before and had solved them then and there – but had he? Surely if the problems had reoccurred then he cannot have removed the root cause. He only applied what he thought were solutions without tackling the root cause. These are often referred to as 'sticking plaster' solutions (Band-Aid in the United States).

Learning Point

When solving a problem, do not jump to Step 4 in the process (Table 13.1) without first evaluating the problem thoroughly.

Attributes Needed for Problem Solving

To be good at problem solving you need to

- Have a clear analytical mind
- Know how to gather facts
- Be able to look for patterns and clues
- Be creative and imaginative
- Be able to relate causes and effects
- Be able to organise change and put solutions in place
- Be self-disciplined to follow the plan
- Be able to explain it all to your colleagues.

In the following Chapters 14 to 19, each of the six problem-solving steps is discussed in detail.

Chapter 14

Step 1: How to Recognise a Problem Exists

SUMMARY

Someone has to make the decision that action must be taken. When everyone is working under pressure, people often work around problems hoping that one day someone will have the time to solve them. This chapter shows how to provide the evidence to justify a break from the norm and to take the opportunity to start making changes.

It is mostly the case that a workplace team tends to be task orientated, focusing on the jobs in hand, and the members will accept the current conditions through familiarity and a reluctance to change. Without regular reviews effectiveness can deteriorate, and it often takes a fresh pair of eyes to recognise the shortcomings that have developed. It is often a moment of inspiration to recognise that a decision must be made and say, 'Houston, we have a problem'.

In any healthcare setting the recognition that there are problems that could be solved and improvements to be made will arise from either an adverse event requiring immediate (reactive) action, as in finding the source of an outbreak of Legionnaires' disease, or from a trend showing a drift towards an undesirable situation such as an increase in the number of falls or a general feeling of dissatisfaction.

Please note, positive trends are important too because conditions must have changed for the better and it is important to know why; for example, people who recovered quickly from being infected with the Ebola virus. Why were they different?

These adverse events can occur either frequently or infrequently and could be, for example

- An adverse inspection report
- A director/manager/supervisor expressing dissatisfaction
- The occurrence of a never event
- A complaint from a patient or their relatives
- A major breakdown of equipment
- Legally enforced changes

Whereas trends, which by definition occur over a longer period of time, could include

- An adverse trend in results; for example, in the National Health Service (NHS) Patient Safety Thermometer
- A buildup of waiting times
- Persistent faults or breakdowns
- Quality control information
- Slow results
- And so on

In general practice the concept of significant event analysis (SEA) is used. The National Patient Safety Agency (NPSA) defines SEA[1] as

'A process in which individual episodes (when there has been a significant occurrence either beneficial or deleterious) are analysed in a systematic and detailed way to ascertain what can be learnted about the overall quality of care, and to indicate any changes that might lead to future improvements'.

Nigel's surgery[2] on the Care Quality Commission (CQC) website gives examples of significant events:

- New cancer diagnoses (good)
- Coping with a staffing crisis (good)
- Complaints or compliments received by the practice (bad or good)
- Breaches of confidentiality (bad)
- A sudden unexpected death or hospitalisation (bad)
- An unsent referral letter (bad)
- Prescribing error (bad)

These types of events fit perfectly into the subject of this chapter.

Sudden Problems and Containment Action

Sudden problems usually include events such as serious complaints, mechanical breakdowns, serious mistakes and unexpectedly bad results. These are the most commonly quoted types of problems, and quality improvement teams are often well practiced in tackling them.

However, one aspect of many problems that often gets neglected or is not dealt with fast enough is the taking of containment action, as might happen after the discovery of faulty breast implants or artificial joints. To do this requires good traceability records to identify the sources. It means making sure the problem does not spread, putting suspect material (or patients) in quarantine, stopping the use of faulty or inaccurate equipment and even suspending a member of staff.

Containment action could also mean putting special quality control measures in place, double checking any results and looking for the specific fault as soon as it can be found. In this situation the root cause must be found and removed, otherwise what was a temporary checking action will become an undesirable permanent addition to the workload. Sometimes during the double-checking action it is useful to gather any background information, the traceability data that can help identify the root causes, the who, what, where and when.

Sometimes it is considered that the best thing to do is to bravely soldier on, but it is not. As I described in the electronic component story, resist the temptation, this is dangerous. Obviously, any immediate patient needs must be satisfied, but afterwards make sure that the deficiency that was being compensated for is flagged up and permanent corrective action taken. Non-conformances such as this must be dealt with quickly. This happened to me in 2008 when the nurse said, 'Oh, this blood pressure monitor has been playing up all day' and proceeded to take a measurement regardless of whether it might be inaccurate. Perhaps this example was not life threatening, but the attitude can spill over into more critical areas.

I have known personally about faulty drips, one of which carried morphine, sounding a warning beeper, none of which caused any concern in the ward whatsoever.

Faulty equipment such as broken beds must not be tolerated, even when equipment is in short supply.

As soon as a problem is identified it is vital that it is contained, and every department should have emergency containment procedures in place that must be followed.

Slowly Developing Problems, Imperceptible Change: Do We Always Know We Have a Problem?

In his book *Most Secret War* (Coronet Books), R. V. Jones[3] quotes an example of the jamming of radar transmissions in World War II. Radio jamming is where transmitters are set up to distort or mask over an enemy's radio signals.

On 11 February 1942, a Colonel Wallace implored the Scientific Intelligence Service to investigate why the Germans were increasing their jamming of British radar. It had increased day by day so gradually that only he had noticed, and he believed there was a reason.

There was a reason. Three German battleships, *Scharnhorst*, *Gneisenau* and *Prinz Eugen*, managed to sail undetected through the English Channel. The German radar officers had subtly increased the intensity of their jamming over a period so that the British would get acclimatised to it without realising that it was becoming so intense that the British radar was useless. I call this 'the law of imperceptible change'. It happens when you do not always realise that a problem exists because the problem has not fully shown itself. Quality control charts are the best way to monitor and detect changes in this type of activity using warning and action limits (see Figure 14.3), but before these can work the normal level must have been measured and calculated. The incidence of bed sores would be a good example for this.

Imperceptible change can occur with malfunctioning equipment that steadily becomes less reliable until it eventually breaks down. It is more effective in the long run to do preventive maintenance than wait for a breakdown.

Imperceptible change can also be difficult to spot when formal reporting is only done infrequently. Imagine waiting for an annual report to find out that some safety statistic had deteriorated badly. Obviously, that sort of change should be acted upon immediately. Sometimes weekly reports can be too infrequent to detect a serious dangerous development. Every important piece of data should be measured and reported on a timescale that is appropriate to the speed and importance of the process.

Trend Analysis

Trend analysis is where an important feature of any work is measured and strict mathematical methods are used to determine whether the results are constant (good) or changing for the worse (bad) or changing for the better (good, but we should know why).

The NHS Patient Safety Thermometer introduced in 2012[4] uses these techniques and is an excellent innovation. It will be even more effective when the techniques have penetrated down to local levels and individual units take ownership of their own results, taking immediate action when necessary. There is a danger, however, that when nationally imposed controls are forced upon local units there is an attitude of 'not invented here', leading to 'alright we'll do it, but only if we have to'. Each participating unit needs to see the value of such a tool and be fully committed to using it as effectively as possible.

A very good example of an improvement trend has emerged in the last 3 years through this Patient Safety Thermometer project. One of the first reports, 'NHS Safety Thermometer National Data Report 2012–2014',[5] was published in August 2014 by NHS England. This has been followed by monthly reports giving results for 13-month periods for the numbers of incidents involving pressure ulcers, catheter and urinary tract infections, venous thromboembolisms and falls. The accumulated results for pressure ulcers from August 2012 to January 2016[6] are shown in Figure 14.1 as a trend chart. A trend line is shown on the chart, as is the formula of the trend line that indicates that the slope of the trend line is 0.0012, that is the reduction

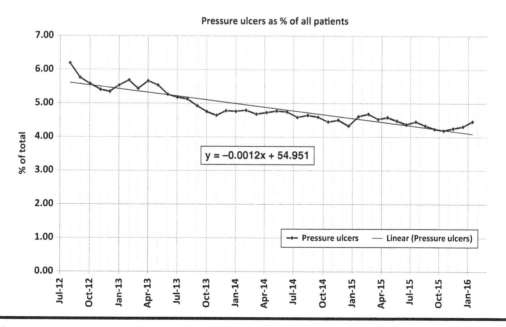

Figure 14.1   Pressure ulcer trend line chart (as originally shown in the data report).

in ulcers per day (y) is 0.0012% or roughly 4.4 fewer patients per 1000 per annum. Given the results are based on roughly 200,000 patients, that represents 800 fewer in the year; that is progress.

(All Patient Safety Thermometer data copyright © 2016, re-used with the permission of the Health and Social Care Information Centre. All rights reserved.)

Trend Charts

There are two features about the line chart (Figure 14.1) that should be noted. First, in scientific convention it is not good practice to have a line chart to represent data points that are not continuous. Each point on this chart represents the value for a month, and any point on the line between months is meaningless. In theory, the data should be represented by a bar chart as shown in Figure 14.2. However, from the point of view of user friendliness, a line chart is easier on the reader's eye and easier to interpret, even though it contravenes strict scientific convention.

The other feature to note is that the *y* axis in Figure 14.1 showing the percentage of ulcers has a minimum value of 0% and a maximum of 7%. This makes the line look flatter than it would if the minimum value on the axis had been say 3.5% and the maximum had been 6.5%. Figure 14.2 uses this set of values for the *y* axis as a bar chart or histogram. What is immediately

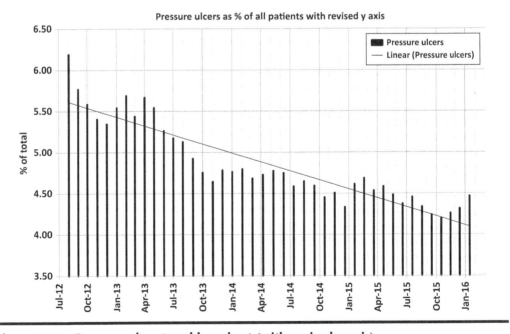

Figure 14.2   Pressure ulcer trend bar chart (with revised *y* axis).

apparent is that the monthly differences are more exaggerated, but there is a need to be careful that the reader does not read more into these differences than is correct. They could be due to normal variability. There are advantages and disadvantages for any set of axis limits.

The 2012–14 report for the Patient Safety Thermometer does claim that there is a real improvement in June 2013, with the period average before then being 5.43% and afterwards 4.72%, an improvement of 13.08% (not 0.71%, the numerical difference between 5.43 and 4.72; the calculation is $(5.43 - 4.72) \times 100/5.43$).

This improvement is not attributed in the report to any specific factor but is most likely due to a general increase in awareness in all the care situations.

In all improvement projects such as this, the next stage would be to look for 'hotspots' and special causes.

Are there any work situations for you where a trend chart would be helpful?

READER EXERCISE

Figures 14.1 and 14.2 show the same data in two different ways; one is a line chart where a line links two adjacent data points. This implies that any point between the data symbols has a meaning. Does it? Try comparing the line chart with the bar chart.

- How often do you think the data was summarised and reported?
- Do you think there is a meaningful improvement?

The report does show how the rate of occurrence of ulcers differs in the different care settings as shown in Table 14.1. The different settings are ranked by number from high to low. The percentage for community hospital wards (8.3%) is higher than the overall average for this data (5.69%) and would be an area to investigate next, as would hospice pressure ulcers at 11.05%.

READER EXERCISE

In Table 14.1, in which setting or settings would you start to 'drill down', that is look for more information about pressure sores in that setting?

As an independent observer, I would judge that three care settings are worth investigating. The community (nationally) is the setting with the largest number of ulcers, 77,731 – a small percentage improvement would

Table 14.1   Analysis of Pressure Ulcers by Care Setting

Care Setting	%	Total	Number
Community (nationally)	5.93	1,310,812	77,731
Community hospital ward	8.30	192,880	16,009
Own home	5.69	261,503	14,880
Nursing home	4.48	150,248	6,731
Mental health ward	1.18	82,300	971
Residential care home	3.42	27,711	948
Hospice	11.05	8,359	924
Other	1.85	40,769	754
Mental health community	0.80	19,578	157
Total	5.69	2,094,160	119,104

help a large number of people. In hospices, the percentage is the highest of all settings – investigating there could highlight a special cause that could be eliminated, but the number of patients who would benefit would be small because the hospice population is only 8,359 out of a total of 2 million.

In community hospital wards the percentage of 8.3%, 16,009 cases is also worthy of analysis and improvement.

The reader should be warned about 'cherry picking' or 'picking the low-hanging fruit' in this type of work. Going for the easy gains is good – good for morale, good politically and, if the improvement team is new, it can be good training in the techniques to use. However, after the easy pickings further improvement becomes harder, and those involved should not become disheartened.

The NHS Safety Thermometer reports show similar results for the other three criteria, namely catheter and urinary tract infections, venous thromboembolisms and falls.

Quality Control Charts

A quality control chart (Figure 14.3) is the specific statistical technique which is used to monitor steady state results, either within upper and lower

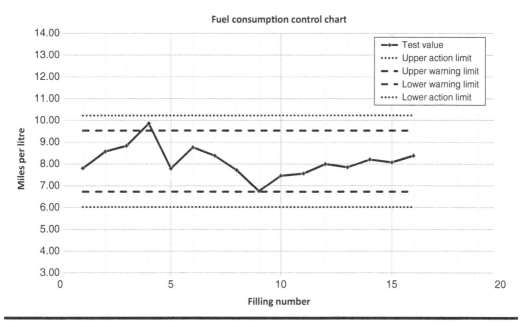

Figure 14.3   Fuel consumption control chart.

warning and action limits or upper limits alone when results must not exceed a maximum value or the reverse when they must not fall below a minimum value.

Figure 14.3 shows the petrol consumption of a 1.6-litre petrol engine over a period of 16 months, calculated after each tank filling. I have chosen this example because it will be familiar to almost everyone.

The results are plotted on a graph, and previously calculated limits are used to trigger action when the data crosses these lines. The warning and action lines are exactly what they say, warning and action. Convention suggests that if three results in succession lie outside a warning line, it is possible that a change has occurred and should be investigated; similarly, if one result lies outside the action line that must be investigated.

Using standard statistical methods (not covered in this book, see books in the recommended reading such as *Measuring Quality Improvement in Healthcare* by Raymond G. Carey and Robert C. Lloyd), the average has been calculated, as have four other criteria – the upper and lower warning limits and the upper and lower action limits. Of the 16 results only one, number 4, is outside the warning limit but within the action limit.

READER EXAMPLE

In the case of the data for petrol consumption in Figure 14.3,
- What could the causes of low mileage per litre be?
- What is the relevance of an upper limit?
- Are there any work situations for you where a quality control chart would be helpful?

In this example, the causes of poor miles per litre could be a soft tyre, an ignition fault or binding brakes.

Very good petrol consumption, as in point 4, can advise the driver how to improve the economy of the car. In this case the good result was obtained on a long motorway journey with few stops.

In the case of pressure ulcers, the data is not 'steady state' because there is a steady improvement (a reduction) over periods of months. However, from a national coordinating viewpoint the data must be monitored, and the chart shown in Figure 14.4 could be used to ensure there is no fall back to the limits prior to January 2015. In that chart, an upper

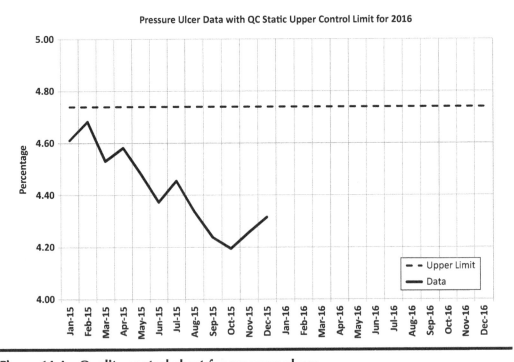

Figure 14.4   Quality control chart for pressure ulcers.

limit for the coming year 2016 has been calculated by the author based on the previous year's (2015) results. But it would only show long-term, slow trends because it is created from data collected across the United Kingdom, and there will be a time lag. Figure 14.4 also does not have a lower limit.

If the coordinators wanted even tighter limits then a sloping upper limit line could be calculated and shown projected into the future, as in Figure 14.5. This would demonstrate continuing improvement.

Unfortunately, as the percentage of ulcers reduces it will become more and more expensive to achieve further reductions, the law of diminishing returns will apply, and it would be realistic to expect the curve to level off horizontal to the x axis of the graph.

Figures 14.1 through 14.5 are for illustrative purposes only and should not be used for any other purpose than learning. (All the data used is reproduced copyright © 2016, re-used with the permission of the Health and Social Care Information Centre. All rights reserved.)

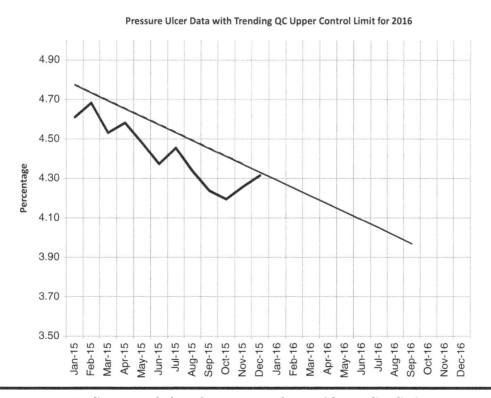

Pressure Ulcer Data with Trending QC Upper Control Limit for 2016

Figure 14.5 Quality control chart for pressure ulcers with trending limits.

Patients' Changing Expectations

Just as the quality of a process output can slowly deteriorate, so patients' expectations can also change, usually requiring higher standards. Referring back to Jennifer's Tale in the Prologue, some people might be surprised at the level of Jennifer's expectations. When I interviewed her I concluded that she is not an unreasonable person; one of her frustrations occurred because when the staff were overworked, it was those patients who shouted loudest and longest who got attention, not those whose need was greatest.

These changing expectations would only be recognised through constant comparison of patient opinion surveys with the organisation's patient care strategy or perhaps through rising discontent. In the following illustration, there was rising discontent among the customers of a pharmacy. This illustration will be used in the next five chapters to take the reader through the six-step problem solving process.

A Problem-Solving Illustration: Poor Service at a Pharmacy

Imagine a small town with two general practitioner (GP) practices and two pharmacies. One pharmacy in particular (named X) appears to be over-worked, and patients/customers complain that there is a very poor service with expressions like, 'They are hopeless', 'They cannot get it right' and so on, vague expressions at the top of the 'Abstraction Ladder' mentioned in Chapter 11. The customers feel they are kept waiting too long, their prescription is wrong or even missing. This perception is ongoing, queues are long and no one appears to be interested in making any improvements. Rumour and dissatisfaction fuel even more rumour.

This has led to both the pharmacy and the GP practice being blamed and given bad reputations in the surrounding area, not necessarily justified. The GP practice would be included in the blame because the patients could think that the prescriptions, for example, were not being transferred electronically to the pharmacy. There is rising discontent with a lack of facts and a great deal of distrust. Where would an improver start?

Preliminary Work

The first step would be to find out what the problems are and gather some data. But who would start the process off? Probably a phone call from the

GP practice to the pharmacy along the lines of 'We have a problem'. Ideally, someone would be delegated, either formally or informally, to start talking to the customers at the pharmacy and asking them whether they had a problem or not. Often in a situation like this those people who would normally just accept the delays would then start coming forward, so the quantity of complaints would start to multiply.

Having assessed the situation, the investigator would start to keep an informal running record of the number of complaints and what the reasons were. This would be informal merely to establish whether the problem was a real one or an exaggeration.

Very quickly it would become apparent that improvements must be made, and the managers concerned would have to start a project. The problem has been recognised, and very quickly the aims can be established: fewer complaints about the pharmacy.

However, those involved, the people at the pharmacy and at the GP practice, are not experienced in this type of work and could start to investigate in a haphazard, unstructured manner. So, how would the formal problem-solving process be used to help them?

The first step in the problem-solving process, 'Recognising that a problem exists', has been notionally established, and a formal start to the project can be made. Ad hoc enquiries have established that there is unsatisfactory customer service at a pharmacy, but that dispensing service includes the GP practice because the practice is part of the dispensing process. The problem has been recognised, but all that the investigators at the exploratory stage have discovered is that there are many rumours and few facts.

Planning Further Action

A joint meeting between the two sets of people needs to appoint an improvement team leader and start to record what needs to be done to achieve an as yet undefined objective.

There then would be enough understanding to start this project. Step 1 in the problem-solving process is almost complete except for the paperwork. This is where a record sheet is used to plan and record actions as shown in Table 14.2.

In this record sheet, there is a set of six sections, one section for each of the steps 1 to 6 of the problem-solving process. In the following Chapters 15 through 19, describing Steps 2–6 of the process, an

Table 14.2 Problem-Solving Record Sheet

Step	Description	Instructions for Record Keeping
		Recognition That a Problem Exists
1	a. Name the problem, put on the improvement list, give reference number	Name: _____ Ref. no.:
	b. Take containment action	Describe the action taken.
	c. Select an improvement leader (and functional representatives if cross-functional)	Leader name: _____ Other team members: Operat'ns / Technical / Sales / IT/Admin
		Getting to the Root of the Problem
2	a. Analyse the problem to identify the core problem	Describe the core problem.
	b. Select a quantitative measure and a target value to monitor improvement / Create Excel spreadsheet	Target value: _____ Units: _____ Excel filename: .xls
		Identifying the Root Causes
3	Brainstorm to identify as many potential causes as possible. Copy to MS Word document	MS Word filename: .doc Create a fishbone diagram showing all potential causes.

(Continued)

Table 14.2 (Continued) Problem-Solving Record Sheet

Step	Description	Instructions for Record Keeping			
		Removing the Root Causes			
4	a. Select the most likely root causes. List them in MS Word document	*MS Word filename:*			*.doc here*
	b. Propose and take steps to remove the root causes	*Confirm the steps taken, when and by whom.*			
			Action taken (Y/N)	*Date*	*Name*
		Method			
		Equipment			
		Software			
		Materials			
		Counselling			
		Training			
		Reorganisation			
	c. Record the action taken on the spreadsheet against the date	*Record made by:*			

(Continued)

Table 14.2 (Continued) Problem-Solving Record Sheet

Step	Description	Instructions for Record Keeping
		Proving a Permanent Improvement
5	Monitor the results, using spreadsheet	*Plot the numerical results on a time-based chart. Excel spreadsheet as 2b above*
		Celebrating Success
6	Close the investigation, prepare report, file the results, celebrate success	*MS Word filename of report:* *.doc* *Leader signature:* *Date:*

extract of each relevant section of Table 14.2 will be shown to illustrate its use for record keeping.

Each of these sections, corresponding to a step, is shown at the end of the relevant chapter following, enlarged and showing fictional data relevant to the illustrative example 'Poor service at a pharmacy'. The complete sheet, Table 14.2, is also a front sheet for the project file that will contain all the documentary evidence of ideas generated, the plan and the work done. This file should be in the form of a project diary and should be supported by visual wall displays that can be annotated with further ideas as they arise.

This complete record sheet is a communication and control tool, used to define the objectives, prevent project creep and inform everyone of exactly what is being done and the progress made. It is also an auditable record of improvements, essential for a correction programme after an independent inspection. The record sheet can also be used to record any changes of project direction should more serious problems be uncovered.

At the planning meeting described, some provisional improvement team members can be appointed. Remember, not much is known about this project, so more relevant people may need to join the team or take the place of existing team members no longer relevant to the specialisms required.

Setting Up the Team

Project Sponsor

The sponsor is usually the most senior person who has the power and knowledge to give support to the leader and the team to get the results needed. He/she will approve project objectives and the project plan. The sponsor should ideally be experienced in using the methods shown in this booklet.

Project Leader

The project leader and the sponsor will be responsible for selecting team members from those departments that operate the process or processes that the improvement will impact on.

The leader will arrange meetings, set meeting agendas, propose objectives, propose the project plan, lead and motivate the team. He/she will identify project setbacks and propose solutions to them.

Project Team

The project team will have a suitable mix of operational experience, leadership and problem-solving skills. They will be cross-functional and will be required to support the aims of the project, keeping their own line managers informed of progress.

People Plan

The project leader must ensure that every member of the team is aware of the tasks in the plan that they will be involved with. Work on the project usually takes the form of

- Meeting at set times to share and discuss results, then plan action. These times must be put in diaries and strictly adhered to.
- Carrying out investigative work between meetings, recording the findings and summarising the results.
- Carrying out major project reviews programmed into a Gantt chart.

The End of the Step

At the end of Step 1, the following progress is recorded:

Step 1a: The problem has been clearly identified and defined, named on a record sheet and added to a master list.
Step 1b: The problem has been contained with special measures.
Step 1c: A leader and an improvement team have been appointed.

Coming back to the illustration problem, 'Poor service at a pharmacy', Table 14.3 is an extracted part of the overall record sheet and has been completed with fictitious data for the delayed prescription problem.

Anticipating Step 6 (Chapter 19) when a presentation (probably PowerPoint) should be given, it is also helpful to write a short narrative to summarise the progress made. Imagine that you will be telling the audience a story of how the project started, what was done at each stage and, finally, the results achieved.

Table 14.3 Step 1: Recognising a Problem Exists

Step	Description	Auditable Record	
1	*Recognising a Problem Exists*		
1a	Name the problem, put on the improvement list, give reference number	*Problem Name:* *'Poor Service at Pharmacy X'* *Initial Project Objective* *'Improved Service, detail to be decided'*	*Ref. no.:* *01*
1b	Take containment action	*Action taken:* *None needed*	
1c	Select an improvement team leader (and functional representatives if cross-functional)	*Leader name: Practice Manager* *Other team members:* *Pharmacist 1* *Pharmacist 2* *Customer representative*	

Step Narrative for Step 1

Project 01: As of [date], the problem name is 'Poor Service at Pharmacy X'; the objective is 'Improved Customer Service (to be defined)'; there is no need for containment action; the Project Leader is the practice manager [name], and two pharmacists [names] and a customer representative [name] are improvement team members. A digital project folder has been created in which to collect all the data and the documentary evidence gathered.

The next action is to move to Step 2 in the process to determine the main reasons for the complaints.

Concluding Step 1: Recognising a Problem Exists

Moving away from the pharmacy illustration and looking at stage 1 in more general terms, after all of the questioning and head scratching you will have either had a problem delegated to you or you will have had ideas for improvement yourself. These will have varying levels of understanding and priority from which you will need to select one specific problem for action, unless, of course, it is very self-evident. How to do this is described in Chapter 21.

You may not know everything about the problem at this stage, but in stage 2 of the process you will set about learning more.

Once you have decided there is a problem to resolve then Step 1 can be completed by appointing a project leader (it could be you) and a group of specialists who can move the work forward. This is sometimes known as a 'task and finish team', which will disband once the improvement is made and confirmed.

The team should then make a record of what has been decided by documenting some very basic information on the record sheet (Table 14.2) previously described and illustrated.

Chapter 15

Step 2: How to Understand and Define the Core Problem

SUMMARY

The nature of the core problem must be clearly stated, documented and communicated. An illustration about delayed prescriptions is used.

What Is a 'Core Problem'?

The core problem is the problem discovered when, after investigation, the team has the clearest understanding about what is going wrong, and a statement can be documented along the lines of the generic statement, '[This is happening that should not be]'; for example, 'Too many patients are suffering from bed sores', 'Too many beds are breaking down', 'Patients have to wait too long at Radiology', 'Too many prescriptions are not ready to collect when expected' and 'Too many records are getting mislaid'.

In the illustration project 'Poor service at a pharmacy', it would be 'There are too many customer complaints'.

Vague Opinions versus Facts

In the early stages of an improvement project it is likely that the problem will be described in vague, emotional terms such as 'too many', as in the previous examples.

An example of this was raised at an improvement team meeting, someone said 'We get too many telephone interruptions'. The response to this should always be 'Bring me facts, not opinions'. The people with this complaint were given that very challenge; they set up a record of interruptions and came to the conclusion that there wasn't really a problem. The method they used was *the tally or check sheet used for counting events*. A slightly more sophisticated example is shown later in Table 15.1. For the reader's amusement, tally marks have been found on bones from some 35,000 years ago, so this technique is well established!

Preliminary Work: Measure, Measure, Measure

To establish the facts, as opposed to chasing rumours, we must 'measure, measure, measure'.

As explained earlier, trend or run charts are used to monitor the changing size or quantity of events that are important. Typical examples from the National Health Service (NHS) Patient Safety Thermometer are falls, pressure ulcers, embolisms and urinary tract infections. Deciding what you need to measure is crucial to making your improvement. Run charts present two types of data, either (1) attributes/whole numbers that are counted, or (2) variables such as body temperature that are measured with an instrument and can have any value on a continuous scale, depending upon the number of decimal places needed; for body temperature that is one decimal place, for example 37.0°C.

The principal use of a run chart is to find out whether the data (parameter) being measured has been increasing, decreasing or staying the same. Sometimes run charts are used to compare the same feature in different locations, usually to decide whether one is better or worse than the other. Obviously, to compare results between settings the method has to be the same. For the data to be accurate, the data collection method must be standardised, consistent and recorded by people who are committed to the process.

For example, when comparing, say, causes of death between countries there may be differences in the way the data is collected, and that makes direct comparison difficult. For comparison purposes it must be 'like for like' and not 'apples and pears'.

Although there may be numerical differences (and there always will be) making one look lower or higher than the other, in statistical terms there might be no significant difference, as decided by statistical analysis.

For example in Table 14.1, in Chapter 14, in the analysis of pressure ulcers, three settings had very similar percentage values – 5.93%, 5.69% and 4.48% compared with an overall average of 5.69%. A statistician would be needed to decide whether the differences are 'significant'. The statistician would use a recognised statistical test for comparing sets of data for significant differences, but these methods are outside the scope of this book.

Unfortunately, someone will always try to see a difference when there really isn't one, especially if there is a political point they might want to prove, sometimes they are 'clutching at straws'. Indeed, there is a cynical saying among quality professionals that the last result is the only correct one and the previous results can be ignored. All measurements will vary depending on the accuracy of the device being used to measure it, and the more accurate the device the more apparent these differences will be.

In statistical terms, these differences will be due to common variation and special variation, terms defined by Professor W. Edwards Deming in 1986. The following tale of the Statistical Baker illustrates this in an imaginary story.

The Statistical Baker

Common cause variation is inherent in every process, but it is not always apparent.

Imagine a professor of statistics who is a keen home baker making bread by hand for her family. She uses the same kitchen equipment every week to make enough dough for five 1 kg loaves. She weighs out the ingredients, kneads them into one large lump, allows it to rise and then divides the lump into five equal pieces to go into the baking tins. After it is baked each loaf will weigh about 1.0 kg, and she will be happy with that. However, having an obsession with statistics, she decides to measure each baked loaf accurately. On the first week, she finds that the lightest loaf weighs 0.91 kg, the heaviest weighs 1.13 kg and the five loaves have an average weight of 1.03 kg. How interesting!

She bakes loaves every week, and after 3 months she has made 65 loaves (13 weeks × 5); the lightest was 0.89 kg, the heaviest 1.15 kg and the average 1.05 kg. She is happy with these results and wonders whether she has now got enough experience to sell the loaves as a commercial venture. In the country she lives in, by law, no 1 kg loaf must be less than 0.85 kg, so most of her produce will be legal.

To think about the implications of this she decides to take a week's holiday break with friends and leave her son to make the family's bread. When she returns she finds that all the loaves average 0.85 kg, and she wonders why they are so light. Worryingly, if she went into business she would be selling underweight loaves. Time is pressing, and she steps back into the home-baking role. On weighing her own baked loaves, the weights are again averaging over 1.0 kg, and she wonders why her son's loaves were lighter.

After carefully questioning the young man she found out what had happened. The plastic bowl she used for weighing the ingredients weighed about 650 g, and he had not tared the weight of the bowl, meaning that the baking ingredients were 0.65 kg lighter, 0.11 kg per loaf. Problem solved.

In terms of statistical variation, when the mother baked the bread she was in control of the process and the variation she measured was common variation. Between the mother and son there was another cause of variation – the fact he did not tare off the weight of the bowl he was using. That was a special cause of variation. A difference to the process had occurred.

In work situations it is important through careful analysis to reduce the variation in the results to a minimum, making the process more repeatable or consistent. One would start this approach by looking for the special causes of variation.

These principles can apply to any situation where measured events are important such as waiting times (minutes), solution strength (mg/l), operating times (minutes) and even blood test results (mg/l) or blood pressure values (mmHg).

READER EXERCISE

Consider you own workplace, and note what data is currently collected.

- Is it about attributes (counted whole numbers) or a variable (measured value with decimal places when appropriate)?
- Is the data shown in graphical form?
- Are there other data that would be meaningful to collect?

Start Measuring and Set a Start Point, a Baseline

Trend data is important for any measurement of patient safety factors.

To be able to demonstrate through measurement that an improvement has been made, a baseline has to be established before any changes to the working methods have been made.

This applies especially to such events as falls, bed sores, waiting times, waiting lists for which you want to see improvement or alternatively, when in control, to watch out for any adverse changes.

Often these run charts should be converted into quality control charts where significant changes can be signalled using calculated warning and action limit lines.

In the early stages of an investigation you may not know exactly what needs to be measured, how it will be measured or who will measure it. This is common, but in the NHS there will probably be a unit somewhere that has tried to do it. Investigate and see if there is a paper published about it from which you can learn, you do not have to reinvent the wheel.

Supposing your work is new, then in preparation for putting your data into a spreadsheet, prepare a data collection form and decide what is to be measured, how, by whom and when. This record sheet does not have to be a permanent feature but should only be used until its appropriateness to the problem has been determined. It could then be replaced by a better method of collecting the data that you and your colleagues decide is important.

The spreadsheet into which the data can be entered will probably be in Microsoft Excel, although other spreadsheets are available. The data can then be analysed and displayed in the most appropriate form. The aim of this display would be to monitor the data to identify how the results are moving, for good or bad.

The next step in this process of measuring and displaying is to decide who in your department would be responsible for monitoring the trends of the important outcomes.

Although to the user it might be obvious what the target of an improvement project might be, it is not always so for an outsider. Sometimes it is necessary on display charts to make a note 'small is good' or 'small is bad' or 'never less than X or more than Y'. It focuses the mind.

In this situation 'significant' has a specific statistical meaning, referring to a result that is not just due to the natural variation but is due to a change in circumstances such as an outbreak of an infection.

What Is Meant by 'Significantly Different'?

British readers might have noticed how each day the news readers report on the BBC that the stock exchange FTSE Index has moved up or down. One day it might be 6 up, another day it is 15 down. The point is 'So what?' Is 6 up or 15 down just normal daily movement, and if so what would a significant change be – 30 points, 50 points, 100 points? We don't know, because we do not know enough about the data.

The same can be applied to rainfall, crime figures, exam pass rates, reported cases of an illness like Ebola virus or malaria and so on.

The numbers reported are nearly always different, but the difference is usually of no consequence because it is just the normal underlying common variation. The difference only matters when the jump is large enough to mean that some new influence or special variation has had an effect. This would be called a statistically significant difference, and it can be shown to be different because of certain calculations that a statistician can carry out.

Always be critical of the early results in an improvement project, and learn about the tests for statistical significance if you want to be able to make any sort of judgement.

In 2000 in England, there was an important criminal case when a family doctor was suspected of carrying out his own form of euthanasia. In court he was found guilty of killing 15 elderly patients.

When in 2001 Professor Baker[1] analysed the time of death of Dr. Shipman's victims he found that there was a significantly different number in the middle of the afternoon from the results of all other doctors, leading him to conclude that these deaths had not been accidental. An inquiry later found that Shipman had probably killed 200 or more patients before he was discovered.

Clarifying the Nature of the Problem

Getting to the core problem is often one of the most challenging parts of problem solving, because when people are interviewed they often have difficulty identifying it and explaining what it is.

Whatever the problem is thought to be, it is vital that the size, extent or seriousness is measured, as in the telephone example mentioned at the beginning of this chapter. This requires some preliminary work, even research, to put some boundaries around the problem. Someone has to be given the job of clarifying it, to find out

- What is happening that should not?
- What is not happening that should be?

Then apply the six magic questions that originated from Rudyard Kipling's *The Elephant's Child*:

> *I keep six honest serving-men*
> *They taught me all I knew*
> *Their names are What and Where and When and How and Why*
> *and Who.*

Suggested Questions	
Place:	What is done? Where is it done? Why is it done there? Where else might it be done? Where should it be done?
Sequence:	When is it done? Why is it done at that point? When might it be done? When should it be done?
Person:	Who does it? Why does that person do it? Who else might do it? Who should do it?
Means:	How is it done? Why is it done that way? How else might it be done? How should it be done?

Your aim when carrying out this diagnosis is to get to the root of the problem. Another technique that can be used is to repeat the questions 'Why is that the problem' or 'So what'. This is known as the *5 Whys*.

Here is a simple example:

THE 5 WHYS

The idea was proposed, 'We need a new computer system'.

Q: 'Why?'
A: 'I can never enter data'
Q: 'Why?'
A: 'The screen takes too long to respond'
Q: 'Why?'
A: 'Accounts department are using up too many screens'
Q: 'Why?'
A: 'They run the payroll on Thursday'
(Note the emotive and vague words 'never' and 'too long')

Using this technique established that the problem is that on Thursdays, and only on Thursdays, there is an overload on the system. The overload is caused by the accounts department making a major computation on that day.

Immediately, ideas can be found for rescheduling the work of both departments to prevent overload on a Thursday. There was no need for a new system.

The Illustration Project: 'Poor Service at a Pharmacy'

The improvement team investigating the problem of 'Poor service at a pharmacy', described in Chapter 14, had completed Step 1. They then needed further information to find the core or, in this case, the most common problem. To do this they needed to gather more information using a record sheet. While doing so they could also ask the six Ws: what, where, when, how, why and who?

A tally sheet would be needed to collect data, but what data should be collected? Does anyone in the team really know how often these problems occur to be able to plan the data collection?

The following list would be a first attempt:

- Date of problem
- Time of problem
- General practitioner (GP)/surgery name
- Nature of problem

The record sheet might look like Table 15.1, only larger than printed here with more space for the data. The table has 14 columns, one for each complaint, which should provide a very good set of data to show what was happening. There is also a check row to show the record had been examined.

Table 15.1   Record of Pharmacy Complaints

Complaint No.	1	2	3	4	5	6	7	8	9	10	11	12	13	14
Date														
Time														
GP name														
Nature of complaint														
Acknowledged														

When enough information has been gathered, the complaints would be grouped into common types and counted for frequency.

After the team had gathered enough information, a more detailed record sheet as in Table 15.2 was created to focus on the most common reasons.

After examining the first 14 complaints, it became obvious that the most common complaint was that prescribed medicines were too often not available or late. To collect more data, six possible causes of delayed prescriptions were proposed and used in Table 15.2 to gather more data.

On this form, the complaint number starts at 15 because it should follow on from the last number used in the previous system in Table 15.1. Remember, reasons for complaints are not necessarily causes. The reason for the complaint may be 'out of stock', but the cause of that could be incorrect stock levels or a national shortage.

The record is titled 'Detailed Record of Pharmacy Complaints' and focuses on reasons for delays, but there is a row to collect information about 'other' types of complaint.

Table 15.2 Detailed Record of Pharmacy Complaints

Complaint No.	15	16	17	18	19	20	21	22	23	24	25	26	27	28
Date														
Time														
GP name														
Nature — Late: Out of stock														
Nature — Late: Missing script														
Nature — Late: Waiting for dispensing														
Nature — Incorrect medication														
Nature — Missing item														
Nature — Other														
Acknowledged														

A completed version of Table 15.2 as shown in Table 15.3 would be needed to condense the data into quantities. It might look like this; the numbers are fictitious.

An Excel spreadsheet can be opened and a chart generated. It would look like Figure 15.1.

This is a histogram or bar chart because, as stated earlier, a line chart should not be used when the data is not continuous, that is each day is a separate set of data and a point between the bars would not have a meaning, there is no data for the time between 1 and 2 February.

The first weekly summary shows that 24 out of 25 (96%) customer complaints were due to what could be called 'delayed prescriptions'. In further detail, 'out of stock' prescriptions amounted to 10 out of 25 complaints (40%). The causes for 'delayed prescriptions' can now be investigated in Step 3.

Self-Monitoring

At this stage of the investigation, it should become apparent to those involved that any of the problematic items listed in Table 15.3 are self-apparent. That is, they are obvious to the people delivering the service. The implications from this are that the pharmacy employees, knowing that

Table 15.3 Weekly Summary of Complaint by Nature

Date		1/2/16	2/2/16	3/2/16	4/2/16	5/2/16	6/2/16	Weekly Total
Nature	Late: Out of stock	2	1	3	1	1	2	10
	Late: Missing script	1	0	1	0	1	1	4
	Late: Waiting for dispensing	1	1	1	0	0	1	4
	Incorrect medication	0	0	1	0	0	0	1
	Missing item	1	1	1	1	0	1	5
	Other	0	0	0	0	1	0	1
Daily Total		5	3	7	2	3	5	25

Number of daily complaints

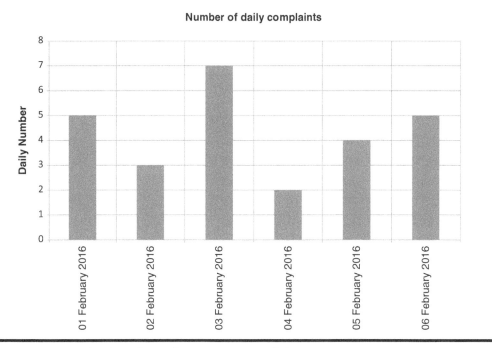

Figure 15.1   Monitoring chart of customer complaints.

these types of problem cause customer concerns or complaints, can count and record each one as it happens. There is no need to wait for the customer to complain. This realisation could be a huge culture change, to take responsibility for anything that upsets customers and stop it at source. It would be the creation of an internal quality control system in which poor quality is identified, and action is taken to prevent reoccurrence. Ideally, a good quality control system stops poor quality before it affects the customer, poor quality is kept in-house and only the employees know about it. The problems would not stop, but they would not impact on customers, and the number of complaints would reduce. This would be a very powerful culture change indeed, but in healthcare it can only be applied in limited circumstances, those in which there is an opportunity to intercept a service.

Concluding Step 2: Defining the Core Problem

In general terms, Step 2, *Defining the Core Problem*, is complete when a statement is prepared and agreed by all, describing the undesirable events, the times when they occurred, where they occurred and who was involved. A desirable outcome (i.e. project success) should be described also.

In the 'Poor service at a pharmacy' example, the core problem is that there are too many occasions when customers do not get their medication when they expect it, for a variety of reasons. In the sample week, 96% of complaints were for this reason. This information is shown in step 2 of the record sheet in Table 15.4.

Reader, please take note, this is a very simplistic example, but it contains all the elements needed to use as a teaching example.

Table 15.4 Record of Step 2: Defining and Confirming the Core Problem

Step	Description	Auditable Record
2	a. Collect data and analyse the problem to identify the core problem	Description: *The major reason for customer complaints is that medication is not available when customers expect it.*
	b. Select a quantitative measure and a target value to monitor improvement Create Excel spreadsheet	Measure: *Complaints per week* Target value: *0 complaints* Excel filename: *prescription_delay.xls*

Step Narrative for Step 2

Project 01: Preliminary investigations have shown that out of 25 complaints, 24 were about medication that was not available when customers expected it. The data is now available in an Excel spreadsheet.

The next action is to move on to Step 3 to determine the main causes of 'delayed prescriptions'.

To tighten the focus of the project the title will now be changed to 'Reducing the number of complaints due to delayed prescriptions'.

Chapter 16

Step 3: How to Identify the Root Causes

SUMMARY

The causes of the core problem must not be guessed but systematically identified using the standard root cause analysis. All analysis work must be documented and publicised. This allows the data to be added to and ideas amended in an open, structured and positive manner.

In Step 2, the core problem will have been identified and documented; examples might be certain records regularly going missing, test results that cannot be found, incidents of 'Nil by Mouth' rules being broken and so on. The next step involves the use of brainstorming to create an 'Ishikawa' or 'fishbone' diagram to identify and record as many of the root causes of the specified problem as considered possible. This is called 'cause and effect analysis'. The original cause and effect diagram was devised by Kaoru Ishikawa in 1968 as a means of structuring and analysing causes of events in the Kawasaki shipyards. Because of the shape, it is more commonly referred to as a fishbone diagram. The basic structure is shown in Figure 16.1, which can be used as a template.

At the head of the fish on the right-hand side there is a box of any shape, in which the undesirable effect is written. The spine of the fish is an arrow, pointing to the head. Feeding into this spine there are four 'fishbones', and at the extremity of each fishbone there is a heading describing a group of similar 'causes'. The four headings normally recommended are 'People',

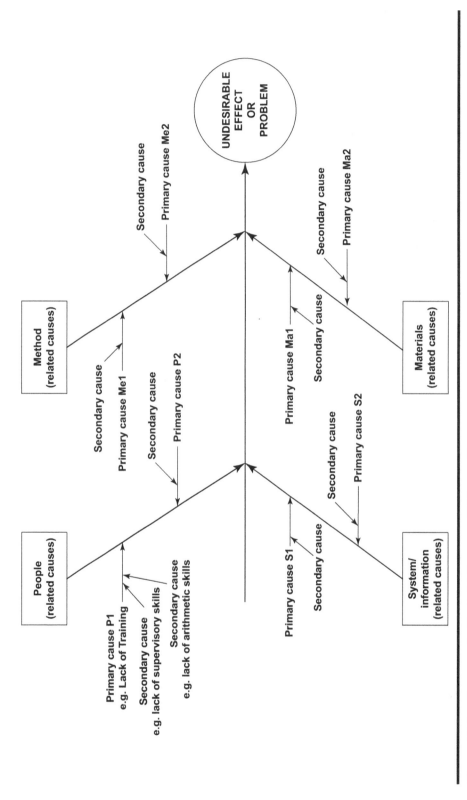

Figure 16.1 Cause and effect, Ishikawa or fishbone diagram.

'Systems/Information', 'Materials' and 'Methods'. Against each fishbone, possible primary causes of the stated effect are lined up in fishbone fashion; in Figure 16.1, eight such primary causes are shown. Sometimes when a possible cause such as 'lack of training' is entered, this can be broken down further and entered as a secondary cause. These might be 'lack of keyboard skills', or 'lack of supervisory skills' and so on. Do not be afraid to put the same cause on two or more different fishbones.

Advanced users of the fishbone method may choose to devise their own group headings, depending on the results of the brainstorming and the nature of the effect or problem being investigated. The tail of the fish can also be used as a fifth grouping.

The purpose of the diagram is to provoke ideas, structure them and display them publicly for further input and comment, in turn provoking more input and discussion. It should be a living document.

At this stage, it is not uncommon for aggressive managers to assert that they know why these things are happening and insist that what they think are root causes be removed. This situation can be managed by responding to the manager's suggestion and monitoring the subsequent results and, if possible, following this problem-solving process as well.

These managers can be even more negative and state categorically, 'It must not happen again', as if the staff could just wave a magic wand to remove the unknown cause.

Brainstorming for Problem Solving

(You might find the term brainstorming unsuitable because of its confusion with some forms of mental illness. If this is so, please use your own alternative expression; idea-storming would be such an alternative.)

Bring a group of lively people around the table, review the evidence and brainstorm the root causes of the problem. Most people are familiar with the principles of brainstorming as a technique in which a leader encourages a group to think of as many ideas as possible on a specific topic in a very short time, writing the results on a flip chart or electronic white board.

Remember the rules of brainstorming:

- Use a flip chart or white board so that everyone can see the ideas.
- Define the ideas sought, for example reasons why prescriptions are delayed.

- Ask for ideas of the causes.
- Do not allow any discussion, it delays the creativity.
- Do not allow criticism, it also delays the creativity.
- Do not filter anything out.
- Write everything down as it is said.
- Explode big ideas into many smaller ones.
- Keep going until you have over 100 ideas.
- Sleep on the results, come back and decide on an action plan.
- Feed the ideas into the fishbone diagram as described in the following section.
- Put the fishbone diagram on public display in an office.

Cause and Effect Analysis: Creating the Fishbone Diagram

Suppose the undesirable effect is 'Reasons why order processing takes too long', this could be in the purchasing section of a chain of care homes. To start brainstorming write the effect as a heading for the flip chart or white board. In this case it would be 'Order processing takes too long'.

After brainstorming, list all the likely causes, group them under the classical, recommended headings 'People', 'Systems', 'Materials', 'Methods' and transfer them on the fishbone diagram at the ends of the diagonal 'bones'.

In the head of the fishbone, enter the effect again, 'Order processing takes too long'.

Stand around the resulting chart and brainstorm further causes to add more detail to the chart. A finished chart for the order processing problem would look like Figure 16.2. All of the entries are possible causes of that effect. The diagram is never finished because new ideas can be added at any time.

There are circumstances when, for a clearer understanding of the causes, different group headings on the fishbones can be used. The next example, Figure 16.3, has been prepared to understand the causes of 'Too many baby deaths before they are 4 weeks old'. For this analysis I have used five groups, 'Attitudes and Culture', 'Mother and Baby Medical', 'Training', 'System and Resources' and 'Research and Knowledge'. Using data derived from various Internet sources including Sands (the stillbirth and neonatal death society)[1], the Office of National Statistics[2] and NHS Wales – 1000 Lives Plus[3], I have created the fishbone diagram shown in Figure 16.3. In this example

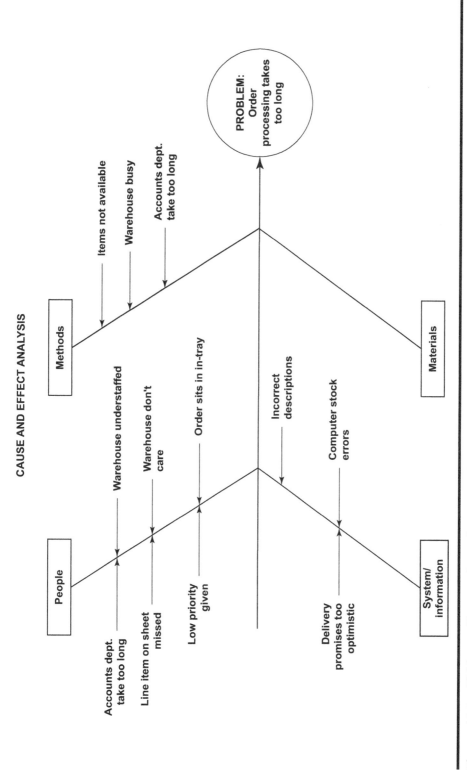

Figure 16.2 Fishbone diagram for order processing.

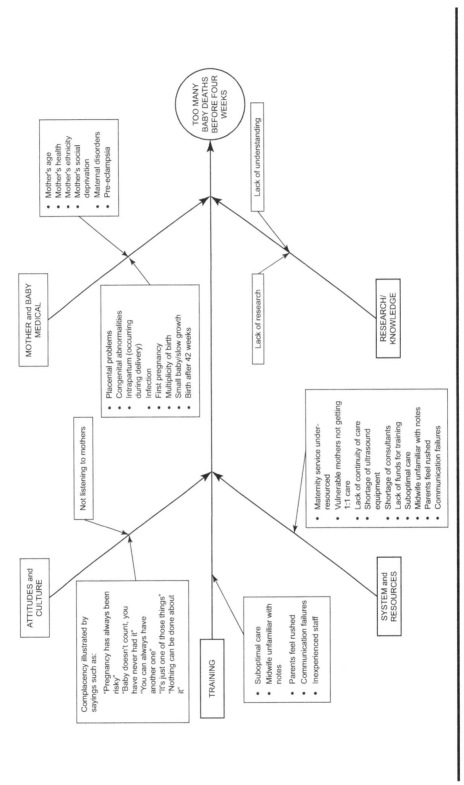

Figure 16.3   Fishbone diagram for early baby deaths.

I have put the possible causes in boxes to show that you can use your own style if you wish to. Another reason for showing Figure 16.3 is to illustrate that this fishbone diagram will lead to others. I could imagine cause and effect diagrams being created for several of the elemental causes in Figure 16.3 such as

- 'Why are attitudes in some baby units so negative and unhelpful'
- 'Why are there so many clinical issues that cause early baby deaths'

and so on.

Each of these possible causes can then be investigated as described in Chapter 17.

The Illustrative Problem: 'Poor Service at a Pharmacy' Now Called 'Reducing the Number of Complaints due to Delayed Prescriptions'

Applying this method to the delayed prescription problem could produce a fishbone diagram as shown in Figure 16.4. For this diagram, different sub-headings have been used, namely four groups of complaint, 'Out of stock', 'Delayed repeats, 'Incorrect medication', and 'Not dispensed or lost'.

This chart was created in Microsoft Visio, a very versatile drawing application. The Visio file can either be printed out directly on A4 or A3 or it can be converted to jpg format and copied into Microsoft Word or PowerPoint for presentations.

Concluding Step 3: Identifying the Root Causes

In general terms, Step 3, *Identifying the Root Causes,* is complete when a comprehensive list of possible root causes has been identified and put on a fishbone diagram. Table 16.1 shows an appropriate record of Step 3 for the prescription problem.

The team will then be ready to start Step 4 of the problem-solving process, 'Removing the Root Causes', selecting those possible causes the team is going to eliminate. Often, Step 4 will run on from the end of Step 3 during the same meeting.

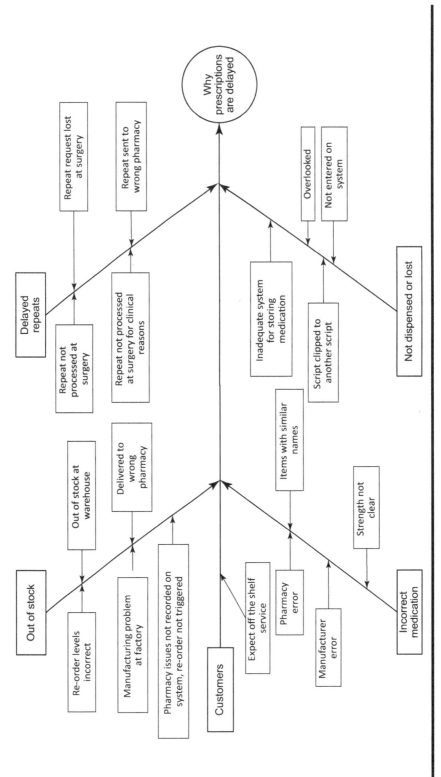

Figure 16.4   Fishbone diagram for delayed prescriptions.

Table 16.1   Record of Step 3: Identifying the Root Causes

Step	Description	Auditable Record
3	Brainstorm to identify as many potential causes as possible. Copy to MS Word document.	Create a fishbone diagram showing all potential causes. MS Word filename: *Fishbone_ prescription delays.doc*

Step Narrative for Step 3

Project 01: A fishbone diagram showing 18 possible root causes of delayed prescriptions has been published and is up in the dispensing room of the pharmacy.

   The next action is to move to Step 4 to take action to remove as many root causes as possible.

Chapter 17

Step 4: How to Remove the Root Causes

SUMMARY

To prevent the problem happening again, the root causes must be eliminated. Permanent changes must be made to the system. People may be retrained, and reorganisation can occur. The organisation has to learn new ways.

Once the cause and effect analysis has been completed, potential solutions can be proposed and a plan of action agreed to remove the most likely causes of the problem.

WARNING

This is the step when many new ideas and opportunities appear. The team should not start to investigate any new problems. They should refer them to the senior manager responsible for the continuous improvement programme, to be put on the list of opportunities, ranked in order of importance and tackled by another team.

As one manager once said to me, 'It is just as important to decide which ideas we are not going to work on until we have solved this one; let's keep focused on the job. If I catch anyone working on a non-priority project ...'

Actions to Eliminate the Selected Root Causes

The first stage in Step 4 is to identify all of the causes which the people on the team can do something about themselves.

In Step 2, a system of measuring the problem should have been set up. This is vital for demonstrating whether the ideas generated in this step are going to be effective, and will act as a baseline for Step 5, 'Proving a Permanent Solution', in Chapter 18.

It is also likely that having published the fishbone diagram to all concerned (remember it was put on a wall), additions could have been made or the descriptions of causes clarified.

Reassess the Fishbone Diagram

The starting point for this step is the fishbone diagram, and for the reader's benefit the diagram for our illustrative problem is shown again as Figure 17.1. The improvement team should prepare a table such as Table 17.1 and list the 18 causes in column B, with each one given a reference number in column A.

Figure 17.1 allows the reader to work between the fishbone repeated from Chapter 16 and Table 17.1.

Evaluation of the List of Possible Causes

The improvement team can now start to analyse the causes, where they probably occur (column D), whether anything can be done immediately to eliminate them (column E) and a notional priority (column F). The notional priority used here is

Priority A: Anything the pharmacy can try to reduce

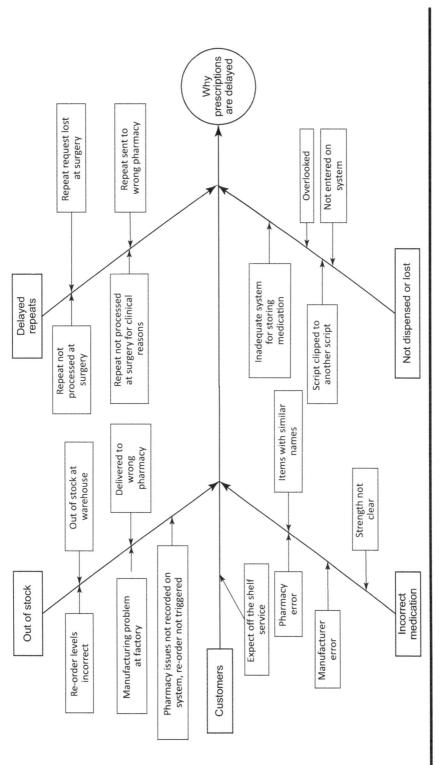

Figure 17.1 Fishbone diagram for delayed prescriptions.

Table 17.1 Root Cause Evaluation and Planning List for 'Delayed Prescriptions'

A	B	C	D	E	F
Ref.	*Fishbone group*	*Cause*	*Where it happens*	*Can the team do something immediately?*	*Priority*
1	Out of stock	Reorder levels incorrect	Head office	No	C
2		Out of stock at warehouse	Warehouse	No	C
3		Manufacturing problem at factory	Manufacturer	No	C
4		Delivered to wrong pharmacy	Warehouse/ Courier	No	C
5		Pharmacy stock issues not recorded, reorder levels not triggered	Pharmacy	Yes	A
6	Customers	Customer expects 'off-the-shelf' service	Pharmacy	Yes	A
7	Incorrect medication dispensed	Pharmacy error, wrong medicine issued	Pharmacy	Yes	A
8		Manufacturer error	Manufacturer	No	C
9		Strength required unclear	GP surgery	Yes	B
10		Items with similar names	Pharmacy/GP surgery	Yes	B

(Continued)

Table 17.1 (Continued) Root Cause Evaluation and Planning List for 'Delayed Prescriptions'

A	B	C	D	E	F
Ref.	*Fishbone group*	*Cause*	*Where it happens*	*Can the team do something immediately?*	*Priority*
11	Delayed repeats	Repeat not processed at surgery	GP surgery	Yes	B
12		Repeat request lost at surgery	GP surgery	Yes	B
13		Repeat not processed at surgery for clinical reasons	GP surgery	Yes	B
14		Repeat sent to wrong pharmacy	GP surgery	Yes	B
15	Not dispensed or lost	Inadequate system for storing medication	Pharmacy	Yes	A
16		Overlooked	Pharmacy	Yes	A
17		Script clipped to another script	Pharmacy	Yes	A
18		Not entered on system	Pharmacy	Yes	A

Priority B: Anything the general practitioner (GP) surgery can try to reduce or a joint action with the pharmacy

Priority C: Anything that must be referred to higher authority for changes to be made.

The reader must define his/her own priorities for each improvement project they undertake.

Table 17.1 provides a pattern for any improvement team to follow, but do not be afraid to make your own amendments, every situation is different.

Start Planning: Agree on an Initial Task List (Gantt Chart)

Having analysed the possible root causes and put more ideas into Table 17.1, it is appropriate to prepare a timed action plan by addressing the priority A items. This plan will contain, for example,

- A set of ideas for action to eliminate the root causes in Table 17.1 or lessen their effect
- A set of well-defined tasks for gathering more data to confirm the overall course of the exercise
- The name of a person to carry out that action and a timescale set for completion of each
- A point where the initial objectives can be confirmed or revised from the early data gathered
- The stage where the effectiveness of the new arrangements is tested in Step 5
- A final sign-off step when the new arrangements are documented and approved for training and dissemination purposes in Step 6
- A presentation to a wide audience to allow them to celebrate the successes, telling the story in Step 6

Put the Plan into a Gantt Chart

A Gantt chart prepared as a table in Microsoft Word is the most common method for publishing the plan. In Table 17.2, column A, on the left, lists the actions, starting with the actions to be carried out first and ending with the final task needed to complete the project. Against each task is a column (B), showing who is responsible for the execution of the detail, while the next column (C) shows who is involved in the activity. In the row for each task a cross marks the week in which the activity must be started, while two crosses in a row denote the period during which the activity is expected to take place, finishing at the final cross, an estimate of the week when that activity should be completed; the cells can be shaded out to highlight them. There will be tasks which cannot be started until a previous task has been completed, this is called a dependent task. There can be a sequence of interdependent tasks, and highlighting them will show the complete path of the dependent activities.

Table 17.2 Project Gantt Chart for Reducing Number of Delayed Prescriptions

A	B	C							
						Timescales			
Task	Resp. of	Involving	Week 1	Week 2	Week 3	Week 4	Week 5	Week 6	Etc. →
Planning meeting to address Table 17.1	JB	Team	X						
Gather data and information	MS	Team	X	XX	X				
Review the data collection for improvement and modify if necessary	TBA	TBA			X				
Review the new data sheet and implement improvements	TBA	TBA					X		
Propose ideas for all priority A items	TBA	TBA			X				
Propose ideas for all priority B items	TBA	TBA			X				
Set objectives for the project using the measures chosen	TBA	TBA			X				
Create and carry out action plan Table 17.3	TBA	TBA			X	XX	XX	XX	To week 8

(Continued)

Table 17.2 (Continued) Project Gantt Chart for Reducing Number of Delayed Prescriptions

A	B	C							
			Timescales						
Task	*Resp. of*	*Involving*	*Week 1*	*Week 2*	*Week 3*	*Week 4*	*Week 5*	*Week 6*	*Etc.* →
Implement new methods	T B A	T B A							To week 8
Propose a date for sign off									X
Test the immediate effectiveness of the new methods	T B A	T B A							Weeks 8–11
Sign off the new methods	T B A	T B A							Week 11
Test the longer term effectiveness in step 5	T B A	T B A							Week 12–13
Give presentation in step 6	T B A	T B A							Week 14

When there are many other dependent sequences (not shown in this example), the longest one can be deduced, and that one will represent the critical path, the rate determining work (see Chapter 9 on critical paths). The project cannot be completed any quicker unless the tasks and resources are changed in the Gantt chart in Table 17.2.

Preparing an Action Plan for the Delayed Prescription Example

Tables 17.1 and 17.2 are the overall plans for an in-depth improvement project to reduce delayed prescriptions.

But what will happen over the first few days and weeks?

The first action the team agreed was to be critical of the data being gathered on the recording sheet to make sure the data would be informative, looking for actual causes created in the fishbone diagram. A person was made responsible for creating a new sheet and for introducing its use by telling everyone how to use it, then reviewing the results after 2 weeks of use.

To start making an immediate impact, the team was asked to select what they believed were the five most likely causes, then to consider action to reduce the chance of each cause having an effect. They chose to investigate the following as shown in Table 17.1.

1. Causes of slow processing of repeat prescriptions at the surgery (causes 11–14)
2. Input of new prescriptions on pharmacy system (cause 18)
3. Medication storage (cause 15)
4. Errors when making up medicines at pharmacy (cause 7)
5. Ways of managing customer's expectations (cause 6)

The action plan the team created is shown in Table 17.3. The action numbers do not reflect parts 1-5 as mentioned previously.

The results of these actions will be to produce changes that will reduce the number of delayed prescriptions.

Each idea will be listed and an implementation plan created. However, before rushing to introduce any permanent changes, consider the effect that the change will have using '*solution effect analysis*', in the 'Other

Table 17.3   Action Plan to Reduce Number of Delayed Prescriptions

Prepared by:	Jo	Date prepared:	February 2016
Ref no.	Action	Resp.	Complete by
Action 1	Modify recording sheet, implement it and report after 2 weeks.	Joe	2 weeks
Action 2	Find out why repeat prescriptions take too long at the surgery.	Chris	2 weeks
Action 3	Why some prescriptions are not put immediately into pharmacy system.	Karen	2 weeks
Action 4	Improve the storage of medication.	Team	2 weeks
Action 5	Look at causes of errors when making medication up.	Karen	2 weeks
Action 6	Find out customer's expectations of the time to receive medication.	Chris	2 weeks

Methods to Use', Chapter 20. This follows exactly the same approach as cause and effect analysis, except it is used to anticipate problems before they happen. It is a form of risk management to prevent undesirable side effects.

The implementation plan for the Delayed Prescription team could be

- Streamline the process for approving repeat prescriptions
- Retrain staff at pharmacy to process new items onto the system
- Change any reorder levels that are out of date
- Devise methods to warn customers when their medication is likely to be delayed.

Managing Project Progress

The project sponsor and the project leader now have a number of documents with which to monitor the progress of the project.

- Description of the undesirable situation, with facts
- Description of a more desirable situation with quantitative aims
- The Project Terms of Reference as set out in the Record Sheet, Figure 14.6 in Chapter 14
- Project Sponsor
- Project Leader
- Project Team
- Project Objective
- A Cause and Effect Diagram
- The Project Gantt Chart showing
  - Tasks
  - Responsibilities
  - Timescales

Progress Limiting Factors

Progress will then be limited by a number of factors:

- The skills of the team
- Time availability
- Self-discipline of team members

Regular Progress Reviews

The project sponsor and the leader must make sure that regular progress reviews are held to ensure that the tasks in the plan are being correctly executed AND the team believe they are making progress towards identifying the improvements that must be implemented.

Assessing Progress

Two questions can be used to assess progress. The first is 'What is the probability that we will achieve the objectives?' When the project starts there is an equal chance it will succeed or fail, so the percentage is 50%. If then the percentage doesn't rise week on week, a complete review is needed to find out what is thought to prevent success. To help this, ask the second question, 'What is the most serious hurdle preventing us finishing this project?' Take soundings from everyone, list the hurdles and see what can be done to overcome them, seeking help from senior management if necessary.

Important Side Issues

It is very likely that during the project many other problems will be identified; this is good. Sometimes the team then adds more actions to its action plan to address these additional opportunities; this is bad. By doing so they are deviating from the project terms of reference, and are in danger of delaying progress on the main project. All additional ideas must be added to the continuous improvement project register (Chapter 21) and must take the appropriate priority.

However, a stark discovery might be made that changes the whole emphasis of the work. This could be something potentially very dangerous with a serious safety, health or financial risk that has not been addressed. In these cases, management action should be taken to reassess the relative priorities of the new finding and the existing project. If this new risk is considered serious enough, stop the existing project in favour of working on the new risk, not forgetting to put the new project on the project register and putting a formal hold notice in the register for the one that has been stopped. Situations like this need very firm management and communication to all concerned.

Unless there is strong leadership and very good communication of the plans, situations like this can descend into chaos and disillusionment.

Concluding Step 4: Removing the Root Causes

In general terms, Step 4, *Removing the Root Causes*, is complete when the action programme has been completed, initial results show that there has been an improvement and at least one of the following has been acted upon to change the working conditions:

1. A new documented method must have been introduced, and/or
2. New equipment must have been installed and be working satisfactorily, and/or
3. New software has been installed and is working, and/or

4. New materials are being used, and/or
5. People have been counselled, and/or
6. Additional training has been carried out, and/or
7. Reorganisation has been carried out, including recruitment

Not only must the people have learned the lessons and changed, the organisation too must have learned.

During all of this time the key measurements used to monitor the occurrence and size of the problem must have been continuously taken.

For the auditable record, Step 4 of the record sheet can be completed as in the following Table 17.4.

Table 17.4 Record of Step 4: Removing the Root Causes/Proposing a Solution

Step	Description	Auditable Record			
4	4a. Select the most likely root causes. List them in MS Word document.	MS Word filename:			*Root causes.doc*
	4b Propose and take steps to remove the root causes.	Confirm the steps taken, when and by whom.			
			Action taken (Y/N)	Date	Name
		Method	*Y*	*March 2016*	*Jo*
		Equipment	*NA*	*-*	*-*
		Software	*NA*	*-*	*-*
		Materials	*NA*		
		Counselling	*Y*		
		Training	*Y*		
		Reorganisation	*Y*		
	4c Confirm from the series of measurements that there is a worthwhile change.	Value at start date =	Value at time of this report =		
	4d Record the action taken on the Gantt chart against the date.	Record made by: *Jo*			

Step Narrative for Step 4

Project 01: Action has been taken to potentially remove five of the root causes of prescriptions being delayed.

The team must now monitor the results and demonstrate that a permanent improvement has been made in Step 5.

Chapter 18

Step 5: How to Prove That a Permanent Solution Has Been Applied

SUMMARY

The problem must not reoccur and this must be demonstrated with measurements before the project is closed.

'One swallow does not a summer make'.

Aristotle

With improvement projects, we want to see differences that are immediately apparent. Having set up a measuring system in Step 2, continue the measurements for enough time to demonstrate that the causes chosen in the plan have been removed, and the target value set at the beginning has been achieved.

To be confident of this, the run chart must show steady values that the team is happy with. Ideally, a statistical test should be done to test whether the results after the introduction of changes are significantly different. There are different attitudes to statistical testing. Many people in business, on one hand, say that any change has to be obvious to be meaningful and that if you have to use statistical methods to prove a difference then the difference is not big enough to matter. In science, on the other hand, when the researcher is looking for trends and relationships, even the smallest of significant differences can be important.

In quality control, when the investigator is looking for consistency and the results start to look different, the investigator wants to know whether to react or not, depending on whether some change or special variation has come into play. The longer he leaves it, the more waste will be produced or damage done.

This book is not a manual on quality control statistics, and anyone needing to understand more about the use of statistics in healthcare is advised to read Measuring Quality Improvement in Healthcare by R. G. Carey and R. C. Lloyd,[1] or Patient Safety by Charles Vincent.[2]

Taking the delayed prescriptions illustration as an example, the method would be as follows.

The records would show either the daily or the weekly number of complaints depending upon the rate at which complaints are being made. It was recommended that you should use an Excel spreadsheet to record the results. One reason for this is that there are tools in Excel to help with the calculations and chart creation.

In Figure 18.1, the results to 2 March 2016 are shown as a histogram. The last recorded complaint was on 25 February, 4 working days before the report.

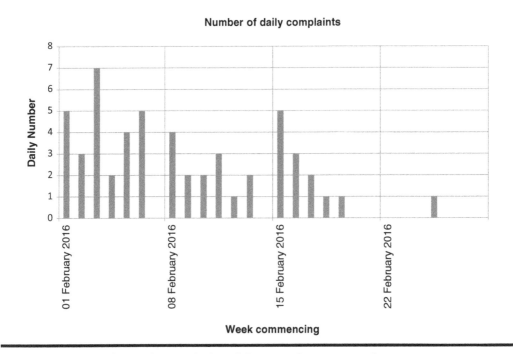

Figure 18.1   Run chart of prescription delays results to 2 March.

The size of the problem has reduced from 4.3 complaints per day to none for 4 days.

This is a fictitious example for illustration purposes only. It shows a histogram, a reducing trend and a condition where instead of stating average number per week, the time since the last complaint can be used as a measure.

Once the target improvement value for a given cause has been reached the team can move onto the next cause.

When an improvement team focuses on a problem, two opposing trends can occur.

When complaint reporting starts, the count often shows deterioration in quality. This is because complaints or problems that previously might have been ignored are 'put into the system'. It is a bit like the manager or leader saying, 'Come on everyone, let's have it all out in the open, put it all on the table'.

Things appear to get worse, this is a good sign because there is more data to investigate, but bad news for the manager because instead of improving, things appear to be deteriorating. Do not be put off!

The opposite effect can also occur. Giving attention to a work process causes the workers to pay more attention to the tasks they carry out and can increase the quantity of work done or improve the quality. This has been named the Hawthorne effect. The term was coined in 1958 by Henry A. Landsberger when analysing experiments at the Hawthorne Works (a Western Electric factory outside Chicago).[3] As soon as a new observer appeared to monitor the work, there was an improvement in output.

As soon as one cause of a problem has been eliminated then another lesser one can be investigated. The improvement team must continue its work until sustained monitoring shows that the original causes of problems have been eliminated or their effect reduced, and the team's objectives have been achieved. Then it will be time to start again with a fresh challenge!

Concluding Step 5: Proving a Permanent Solution

In general terms, Step 5, *Proving a Permanent Solution*, is complete when the target result has been reached and held for an agreed time. The team can complete the record sheet as shown in Table 18.1 and move on to Step 6.

Table 18.1 Record of Step 5: Proving a Permanent Solution

Step	Description	Auditable Record
5	Monitor the results, using spreadsheet.	Plot the numerical results on a time-based chart. Excel spreadsheet as in Step 2b record.

Step Narrative for Step 5

Project 01: Having introduced five changes to the pharmacy system, customer complaints have been reduced from 27 in week commencing 1 February 2016 to one in week commencing 22 February 2017. Monitoring will be continued.

A presentation of the results will be given on 30 April 2016.

Chapter 19

Step 6: How to Close the Project and Celebrate Success

SUMMARY

Enjoy the fact that something has been achieved, and then formally close the project and disband the team.

Signing Off Completed Projects

Signing off a project on completion is essential for ensuring that the original objectives have been satisfied and for the overall health of the entire programme.

It is the responsibility of the sponsor to decide when a project is complete by testing the results.

Test the Results

Completion should be confirmed by testing the outcome. Has the desired change been achieved for a sustained time period? Has the new process been introduced satisfactorily? Whatever the plan was, did it happen; was it effective? Was the project objective achieved?

Remember the list of possible changes quoted in Chapter 17? Has one of these or something very similar happened, and has it worked to permanently achieve the objective?

- A new documented method must have been introduced, and/or
- New equipment must have been installed and be working satisfactorily, and/or
- New software has been installed and is working, and/or
- New materials are being used, and/or
- People have been counselled, and/or
- Additional training has been carried out, and/or
- Reorganisation has been carried out, including recruitment.

As Charles Vincent found from the work of the researchers Tucker and Edmundson (quoted in Chapter 11),

> *The very ingenuity and resourcefulness that are rightly admired in clinical staff, and that produce immediate benefits for patients, can inhibit more fundamental organisational change.*

In other words, the organisation and the system must learn lessons too.

Stop Project Creep

Whatever the outcome, it is essential not to extend the project to achieve changed targets; otherwise 'project creep' will start. Project creep, like 'moving the goalposts', prevents the team from recognising true progress and 'sealing the improvement into the system'. Instead, it drags the project out and can cause the project to seem to go on forever.

Celebrate Success

Organisations are only too ready to criticise bad work, it is just as important to praise good work. This step could be called either 'Celebrating Success' or 'Recognising Success'. It does not matter, because the important point is that everyone involved knows the task is completed and gets the 'good feeling' that comes from completing work successfully.

There are a number of ways of doing this:

• Writing a report
• Filing all the data
• Giving a presentation, PowerPoint is useful
• Giving a prize to the participants and thanking them for their efforts
• Receiving a letter of congratulations from a director/sponsor

The report, as well as giving the participants some pride in the work, will also provide a permanent record of the problem and how it was tackled. This could be very valuable in the future for reference purposes. The report should contain

• A statement of the problem
• A collection of the data
• Any charts produced, process maps, cause and effect diagrams
• The action plan and a record of the action taken
• The results achieved
• Names of the participants
• A signature of approval from a director/sponsor

The five Step Narratives created at the end of each of the previous steps can be used as the basis for the presentation, and on that principle a PowerPoint presentation could be completed with six slides only.

After the presentation, the team *must* be formally disbanded. It is all too easy to recall a side issue to work on. If the other issue is important enough then a new project should be started, from Step 1 of the process.

Completion of Step 6: Celebrating Success

In general terms, Step 6, *Celebrating Success*, is complete when a report has been written, the data has been filed, a celebration has been held and the team has been disbanded. The Step 6 record is shown in Table 19.1.

The problem-solving process record sheet will now be complete.

A blank version of the final record sheet is shown in Figure 19.1.

Table 19.1   Record of Step 6: Celebrating Success

Step	Description	Auditable Record
6	Close the investigation, prepare report, file the results, celebrate success.	MS Word filename of report: *Delayed Prescriptions.doc* Leader signature: Director/Sponsor signature: Date:

Step	Description	Instructions for record keeping				
		Recognition that a problem exists				
1	a. Name the problem, put on the improvement list, give reference number.	*Name:*			*Ref. no.:*	
	b. Take containment action.	*Describe the action taken*				
	c. Select an improvement leader (and functional representatives if cross functional).	*Leader name:*				
		Other team members:	*Operat'ns*	*Technical*	*Sales*	*IT/Admin*
		Getting to the root of the problem				
2	a. Analyse the problem to identify the core problem.	*Describe the core problem:*				
	b. Select a quantitative measure and a target value to monitor improvement. Create Excel spreadsheet.	*Target value:* *Units:* *Excel filename:* *.xls*				
		Identifying the root causes				
3	Brainstorm to identify as many potential causes as possible. Copy to MS Word document.	*MS Word filename:* *.doc*				
		Create a fishbone diagram showing all potential causes.				
		Removing the root causes				
4	a. Select the most likely root causes. List them in MS Word document.	*MS Word filename:* *.doc here*				
	b. Propose and take steps to remove the root causes.	*Confirm the steps taken, when and by whom.*				
			Action taken (Y/N)	Date	Name	
		Method				
		Equipment				
		Software				
		Materials				
		Counselling				
		Training				
		Reorganisation				
	c. Record the action taken on the spreadsheet against the date.	*Record made by:*				
		Proving a permanent improvement				
5	Monitor the results, using spreadsheet.	*Plot the numerical results on a time-based chart.* *Excel spreadsheet as 2b above*				
		Celebrating Success				
6	Close the investigation, prepare report, file the results, celebrate success.	*MS Word filename of report:* *.doc* *Leader signature:* *Date:*				

Figure 19.1   Complete Six-Step Record Sheet.

Chapter 20

Other Methods to Use

SUMMARY

Examples of further techniques that could either trigger an idea or help solve your problem are shown.

As illustrated earlier, many problems automatically require specific methods to solve them, especially those involving timescales or mistakes.

Timescales

Any problem involving timescales, that is, slow processes, will require analysis of the process using process mapping, and then trend charting to measure the current time parameters and the effect of any subsequent changes. Once a specific process step is identified as slowing the process down (a rate-limiting bottleneck), root cause analysis will help identify the causes.

Mistakes

Similarly, any problem caused by mistakes should be analysed using the root cause analysis method.

Methods Already Described

A prescriptive approach is not infallible, and every problem should be examined in its own right. There are a number of basic improvement techniques which should be in everyone's armoury and which can be used at the appropriate step of 'the problem-solving process'.

The list of items already covered is shown in the following Table 20.1, and the methods are grouped according to whether the primary use is for analysing problems (A) or alternatively, when planning investigations or taking remedial action (P). Whenever you have a problem, looking through these different techniques could trigger an idea for solving it.

Table 20.1   Methods Already Covered

Method	*Type*	*Purpose*	*Where in Book*
The problem-solving process	A	Ensures a systematic approach to solving problems.	Chapter 13
Process mapping	A	Understanding work processes.	Chapter 9
Identifying the critical path or bottleneck	A	Helps to speed up a process.	Chapter 9
Analysing and clearly stating the problem	A	Communicates the problem clearly.	Chapter 11
Histograms	A	Data presentation.	Chapter 14
Run or trend charting	A	Monitoring trends and progress.	Chapter 15
The Five Whys	A	Gets to the real opportunity.	Chapter 15
Tally or check sheets	A	Counting and analysing events.	Chapter 15
Cause and effect	A	Finding the root causes of a problem.	Chapter 16
Brainstorming	P	Seeking ideas.	Chapter 9

Table 20.2   Other Methods Not Covered

Method	Type	Purpose	Method
Scatter plan/map	A	Analysing events in two dimensions (plan form), looking for causes.	1
Pareto analysis, the 80:20 rule	A	Finding the 80% of effect from 20% of causes.	2
The 5 Ss	P	Improving housekeeping and workflow.	3
Force field analysis	P	For reducing resistance to change.	4
Priority rules	P	Ensuring best use of time when under pressure.	5
How2	P	Avoiding negative attitudes.	6
Paired comparisons	P	Making a choice.	7
Decision trees	P	Selecting the best course of action for repetitive situations.	8
Overcoming negativity	P	Used when discussing change.	9
Solution effect	P	Anticipating problems when planning change action.	10
2 x 2 matrix	A	Analysing situations.	11
Reflective listening	A	Helping to establish people's thoughts in interviews.	12

Other Methods

There are many more methods that can be used in problem solving, and a selection is given in this chapter. They are listed in Table 20.2.

Method 1: Scatter Plan/Map

Type of problem that this method is useful for – analysing events in two dimensions when looking for causes:

'Reports have been made of rodents chewing vital electrical cables. Create a scatter diagram of damaged cables and sightings around the buildings, both before and after setting traps'.

A scatter plan or map can be used, for example, to show where on the plan there are clusters of outbreaks, thus guiding investigators to look for causes associated with the location.

One of the first scatter diagrams was made by Dr. John Snow in 1854 to show the incidence of cases of cholera in central London around a public water pump that had been sunk too close to a cesspit in Broad Street, Soho. The council responded by removing the pump handle. The central portion of John Snow's original is shown in Figure 20.1, where each household affected is shown as a black mark.

A scatter plan could be of a building, or a room, a county map or the outline of a human body, depending upon the nature of the problem.

This meaning of scatter plan or map should not be confused with the plotting of x and y numeric data on a scatter plot to look for a mathematical relationship.

Method 2: Pareto Analysis; the 80:20 Rule

Type of problem that this method is useful for:

'How would we find out the best way of reducing the cost of missing stock in the stores?'

Pareto analysis is used in problem solving to find the fewest causes that are creating the largest number of adverse events. By eliminating these few causes, a large number of problems will be prevented. The method is named after the Italian economist Vilfredo Pareto who in 1896 found that 20% of the population owned 80% of the land. This principle holds true for many other things.

In healthcare, this method can be applied to any situation where there are multiple adverse events such as medication errors, lost reports, complaints, pharmacy problems, infection outbreaks, falls and so on.

The following example is a fictitious one from the warehouse of a large healthcare organisation. When auditors came to value the stocks in the warehouse, the actual number of items in stock did not agree with the computer stock control values. Many items were missing, possibly because they were either incorrectly entered on the computer or stolen. The items with discrepancies were analysed, and the results are shown in Table 20.3, in which

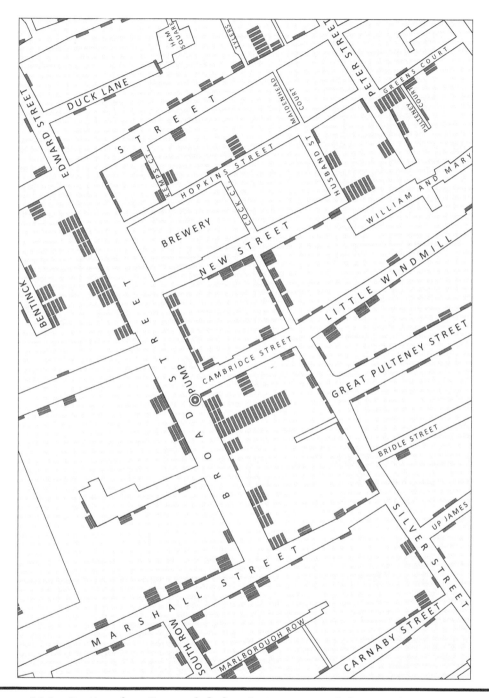

Figure 20.1 Scatter plan: Cases of cholera in 1854 around the Broad Street pump, Soho. (Image courtesy of Wellcome Images, Wellcome Collection, London).

Table 20.3   Stock Items Ranked by Number Missing

Item	Cost per Item Type £	Number of Missing Items			Total Cost per Item £
		Number	% of Total Number	Cum % by Number	
A. Small notepads	0.20	436	45.2	45.2	87.20
B. Pencils	0.20	277	28.7	73.9	55.40
C. Boxes of gloves	2.60	128	13.3	87.2	332.80
D. Pens	0.50	55	5.7	92.8	27.50
E. Calculators	5.80	44	4.6	97.4	255.20
F. Notebooks	2.00	22	2.3	99.7	44.00
G. Storage boxes	0.70	2	0.2	99.9	1.40
H. Protective goggles	1.00	1	0.1	100.0	1.00
TOTAL					804.50

the missing items are ranked by quantity missing. The greatest discrepancy was for small notepads – 436 were unaccounted for. Pencils were next with 277 missing, and so on down to one pair of eye protection goggles. Each type of item is coded with a letter from A to H in descending order.

Table 20.3 shows that 87.2% of the missing items, by number, came from three fault categories (A, B and C). This is calculated by cumulatively adding the totals missing and putting the cumulative percentage in the fifth column. A total £804.50 worth of material is unaccounted for, and the warehouse manager has been told to reduce the cost of losses.

But ranking the missing items by number missing is not the best way to approach this particular problem. At first glance, reducing the number of A, B and C items that go missing can only save £475.40, which is more than 50% of the losses. However, suppose the coded items were ranked by the cost of the loss, how would that look?

Using Microsoft Excel the list can be sorted by the total cost of each type of item in column 6, these results are shown in Table 20.4 and graphically in Figure 20.2.

Table 20.4   Missing Items Ranked by Cost of Items Missing

Item Code	Cost per Item £	Number of Missing Items	Cost of All in Item Code £	Cumulative Cost £	£ %
C	2.60	128	332.80	332.80	41.37
E	5.80	44	255.20	588.00	73.09
A	0.20	436	87.20	675.20	83.93
B	0.20	277	55.40	730.60	90.81
F	2.00	22	44.00	774.60	96.28
D	0.50	55	27.50	802.10	99.70
G	0.70	2	1.40	803.50	99.88
H	1.00	1	1.00	804.50	100.00

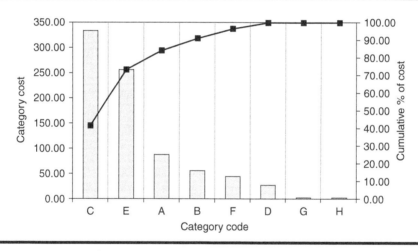

Figure 20.2   Pareto analysis.

This method of ranking shows that 83.93% (£675.20) of the cost of losses comes from only three items, C, E and A. The warehouse manager only has to investigate why boxes of gloves, calculators and small notepads go missing and stop it to save the bulk of the cost.

Imagine a similar, but non-financial exercise to investigate medication errors in which possible errors could be dose missed, wrong time, wrong drug, overdose, wrong patient and so on.

Perhaps there is a problem in your department that deserves investigation?

Method 3: The 5 Ss

Type of problem that this method is useful for:

'The pharmacy stores is becoming very untidy, and it is sometimes difficult to find some items, wasting people's time'.

The 5 Ss (five esses) method is what we often call 'A place for everything and everything in its place'. Any work will proceed more quickly if everything that is needed is immediately to hand, ready to use and not hidden by unnecessary items as could be left behind by the previous worker including empty coffee cups and pizza boxes.

The method is called the 5 Ss because it is carried out in five steps, Seiri, Seiton, Seiso, Seiketsu and Shitsuke, which translated from the Japanese means Sort, Straighten, Shine, Standardise and Sustain.

Imagine that the work area to be improved is a chemical solution preparation area. It uses sterile solutions and sterile vessels. Once made, the solutions are chemically tested for strength. Raw materials are kept refrigerated, as is the final product.

Suppose that a problem of contamination has occurred, and the manager wants to overhaul the whole area by using the 5 Ss method.

Step 1: Sort

The purpose of 'sort' is to remove what is not needed and keep what is, very similar to what some call de-cluttering.

For the record, it is a good idea to take some photographs for a 'before and after' presentation.

To decide what is needed and to be kept, refer to the work methods used in that area. These should read like a well-written cooking recipe in which the utensils, the ingredients and the larger pieces of equipment are listed, followed by a step-by-step description of the method.

Because the work area being improved is not a kitchen but a chemical preparation area, then the utensils become the chemical mixing aids. The ingredients are the chemicals used to make the product. The recipe is the method used to prepare the mixture. The oven becomes the cold storage and so on.

In an office area, there are equivalents also. Paperwork coming in is sorted, data is processed and information is passed on using telephones, computers, tablets and word of mouth.

In carrying out this analysis, the thought processes employed are very powerful in that they help those involved to strip their work methods down to the basic essentials.

A useful analogy that can be used to help understand this is the 'Motorcycle Paramedic' who only has a relatively small pannier box for his or her emergency equipment. He/she will have decided exactly what the box must contain to be available for 95% of the emergencies he/she has to attend. Similarly, use those same criteria for what must be available in the chemical preparation area.

Now double check that everything that is not needed has been removed. Starting at one end of the process area, look in cupboards and empty them. Look on window sills and clear them. Look on shelves and clear them. It is strange how after several years doing the same job, clutter becomes camouflaged and invisible to the people around it.

The wife of a friend of mine had a good method. She would go through whatever room or cupboard that needed de-cluttering and put the clutter she intended to throw out by the outer door. She would then say to her husband 'If there is anything there that you want to keep, take it now, otherwise it all goes out!'

Another area for consideration is 'desk drawers'. Desk drawers are just as much the organisation's property as anywhere else, and managers should have the authority to inspect these to ensure that only work-related matter is held in them. There is an argument that drawers are unnecessary – if they contain tools or data then those items should be on the worktop, visible and available.

Now have a look at the walls, doors and windows. Take down all notices, scraps of paper, photographs, personal calendars and jokes that were amusing at the time. Avoid falling into the trap of keeping things 'just in case'. Ask the question 'Just in case what?' Then ask 'How often is that likely?' Only then, if the answer is a genuine probability, put the material in a box labelled 'To be used in the case of …'.

Put all the 'stuff' that is not needed outside the area and decide whether it is to be stored elsewhere, recycled or thrown out. At this stage, remove as much as possible.

Take another set of photographs.

Step 2: Straighten

Now design your workspace. Having identified the equipment and materials that are essential to the process, it is now time to decide where to keep them so that they are readily to hand.

If waste is produced during work, identify how and where it is to be collected.

Have a specific place for everything, within reach when it is needed.

If floor positioning or storage is needed, mark it out. This is where silhouette peg-boards can be useful. Each implement has a hook on the board with a painted silhouette under it. When the implement is being used or missing the silhouette is visible, simple but effective.

On the walls, put back important up-to-date information that is referred to hour by hour. Agree on any pleasing or motivating décor such as framed pictures. Even take the opportunity to call in the decorators.

Then when you think the layout is the best you can think of carry out some trial runs, involve everyone who does the work and ask their opinion for further improvements.

Finally, take more photographs, both as a means of showing others how the method is used and as a set of visual standards for 6 months' time when comparisons can be made to ensure that the standard is being maintained.

Step 3: Shine

Every day, maintain a high standard of cleanliness. Clean and polish around every workstation to a schedule or routine. Applying the 5 Ss method to the cleaning, you will need a designated area for cleaning equipment that is just as orderly as everywhere else. Unfortunately, cleaning material storage cupboards become a dumping ground for rubbish. Don't let that happen.

There are large businesses that have a clean desk policy. In these companies the cleaners have the authority to throw out anything that is left behind on a desk at the end of the day or shift.

Again, remember the slogan 'A place for everything and everything in its place'.

Step 4: Standardise

Steps 1, 2 and 3 have now set the standard for the workplace, and those working in it have now to decide how to maintain it that way – it has to be sustainable. Use the photographs and carry out self-audits.

Watch out for 'invaders', people or objects that surreptitiously appear on benches, tables or desks. Also watch for items that mysteriously disappear into drawers, lockers or other departments. Continuously strive to make the workspace tidy and efficient.

Step 5: Sustain

Make everyone accountable for the tidiness and appearance of the area. Give everyone the authority to maintain the agreed standard, and every day, week and month repeat the Sort, Straighten and Shine. If in doubt go back to Step 1, Sort.

Finally

We started with a chemical preparation area, and now after the 5 Ss have been applied the essential tools and equipment will be readily available, as will the raw materials, stored as necessary. Finished solutions will have been tested and will be stored correctly. All of the essential records will be safely and systematically stored with easy and quick access.

No unnecessary materials will be anywhere to be seen, and everywhere will look very clean, tidy and efficient. Job done, a place for everything and everything in its place.

Method 4: Force Field Analysis

Type of problem that this method is useful for:

> 'We want to implement an online appointments system as quickly as possible. What precautions do we need to take?'

In force field analysis, which is often suitable for planning step changes such as implementing an online appointments system, the driving and restraining forces affecting a given objective are determined. Then work is carried out to first reduce the restraining forces which reduce the resistance to the change and then enhance the driving forces to help push the changes through. The example is self-explanatory but by no means complete (Figure 20.3).

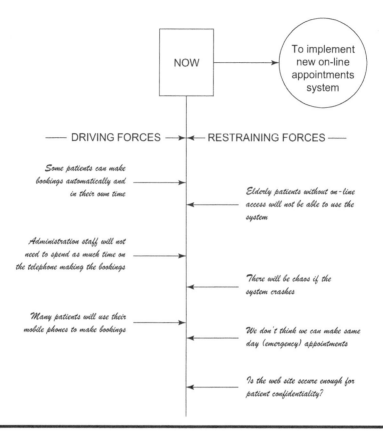

Figure 20.3   Force field analysis.

Method 5: Setting Rules for Priorities

Type of problem that this method is useful for:

> 'The staff in the engineering department find they are being pulled in all directions by unclear priorities. Can this be made less stressful for them?'

This technique is used to state the sequence in which work is going to be done according to an agreed set of priorities. It is a potential solution to problems where important work is neglected and less important work is done instead. It can be a method to overcome the situation where priority is given to the person who shouts last or loudest.

It can be used, for example, in 'repair work prioritisation'.

Codes for Repair Work Prioritisation

In a hospital repair workshop, work arises from a number of different sources and management have decided that tasks must be done in the following sequence:

Priority code 1: Surgical theatre breakdowns
2: Intensive Care breakdowns
3: General ward breakdowns
4: Routine maintenance
5: Research laboratory

(This is only an example; it is not a recommendation!)

As new work comes in, the work request (all workshop requests should have a request form for communication, costing and planning) is given a priority code put on the appropriate pile.

This is very similar to triage prioritisation.

If your department needs to use this method you must analyse the alternatives very carefully, even consulting the recipients of the service to make sure the priorities have their agreement.

Method 6: 'How to' Turning Negatives into Positives

Type of problem that this method is useful for:

'When we have been problem solving a lot of people can only see the downside of issues. How can we be more positive?'

Negative attitudes can range widely between 'Why bother' or 'It's not my job' to much more subtle responses such as diversionary tactics. Often the people displaying these negative attitudes are quite unaware of how their responses appear to other more positive people. Watch out for this happening, and challenge the person with an expression such as

'Please don't tell me why we can't do that, tell me how we can make it possible'.

When exploring improvements to working practices instead of stating the problem, explain the improvement in the positive sense by starting the sentence with 'How can we ...?'

This is called the How2 approach.

Example

A given idea can be expressed either negatively or positively as follows:

'It takes too long to process test results' (negative)
or
'How can we process test results faster?' (positive – the How2 response)

Napoleon Bonaparte is reputed to have said to his generals, 'Don't bring me problems, bring me solutions'.

Method 7: Paired Comparisons

Type of problem that this method is useful for:

'We have to choose new furniture for the office. How can we make the very wide choice easier?'

Making choices: If during the course of planning choices have to be made between competing items, it can be useful to put the alternatives in a list and then pair them off, then eliminate one from each pair.
Suppose you have to choose between four cars A, B, C and D.
A and C are the same colour,
B and D are similar for another reason.
Go through these steps:

1. Eliminate by choosing the best between A and C
2. Eliminate by choosing between B and D
3. Then compare the two winners and make the final choice.

Method 8: Decision Trees

Type of problem that this method is useful for:

'In the maintenance department, we have found that some technicians are quicker than others at finding faults. How can we document their methods so that we can train others?'

It can be very beneficial to adopt a prescriptive approach to investigations to make sure that they are done in the right sequence and that important steps are not missed. The flow chart showing how to do this is called a decision tree; an example is shown here for repairing a TV set (Figure 20.4).

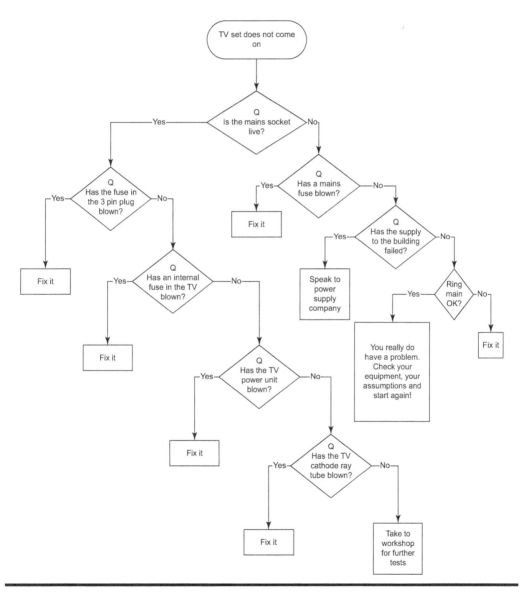

Figure 20.4   Decision tree for TV power failure.

Method 9: Overcoming Negativity. How NOT to Kill a Good Idea

Type of problem that this method is useful for:

'Many of the people in our department are very reluctant to change and are good at prevaricating. How can we watch out for this?'

This is a form of negativity that could be used by any person who is afraid of change will come up as reasons not to try something new.

Put this chart on the conference room wall, and whenever one of the tactics is used draw the person's attention to it.

This list is just one of many similar ones around on the Internet.

DO NOT TRY TO KILL GOOD IDEAS THIS WAY!

1. See it coming and quickly change the subject.
2. Ignore it. Dead silence intimidates all but the most enthusiastic.
3. Feign interest but do nothing about it. This at least prevents the originator from taking it elsewhere.
4. Scorn it. 'You're joking, of course'. Make sure to get your comment in before the idea is fully explained.
5. Laugh it off. 'Ho, ho ho, that's a good one, Joe. You must have been awake all night thinking that up'.
6. Praise it to death. By the time you have expounded its merits for 5 minutes, everyone else will hate it.
7. Mention that it has never been tried before. If the idea is genuinely original, this is certain to be true. Alternatively, say, 'If the idea's so wonderful, why hasn't someone else already tried it?'
8. Say, 'Oh, we've tried that before', even if it's not true. Particularly effective with newcomers. It makes them realise what complete outsiders they are.
9. Come up with a competitive idea. This can be a dangerous tactic, however, as you might still be left with an idea to follow up.
10. Return it to sender with:
    'You need to be much more specific about your proposal'.

11. Stall it with any of the following:
    a. 'We're not ready for it yet, but in the fullness of time ...'
    b. 'I've been wanting to do that for a long time, but right now ...'
    c. 'Let's wait until the new organisation has settled down ...'
12. Modify it out of existence. This is elegant. You seem to be helping the idea along, just changing it a bit here and there. By the time the originator realises what's happening, the idea is dead.
13. Try to chip bits off it. If you fiddle with an idea long enough, it may fall to pieces.
14. Make a strong personal attack on the originator. By the time he or she has recovered, the idea won't seem so important.
15. Appoint a committee to sit on the idea. As someone once observed: 'A committee is a cul-de-sac down which ideas are lured, then quietly strangled'.
16. Drown it in cold water. As in, 'We haven't got the staff to do it ... the intangible risks would be too great ... that's all very well in theory, but in real life ...'
17. If all fails, encourage the originator to look for a better idea. Usually a discouraging quest. If he or she actually returns with one, start them looking for a better job.

Method 10: Solution Effect Analysis

Type of problem that this method is useful for:

'We need to make some changes to the layout of the waiting rooms. How can we avoid problems during and after the process?'

In solution effect analysis, the team brainstorms what the consequences might be of implementing a certain solution, producing a diagram similar to a fishbone but, by convention, pointing right to left. If these consequences are likely to have an adverse effect, methods can be devised to counter it. This is a method to anticipate problems before any permanent changes are made. It can also be used to compare different solutions (Figure 20.5).

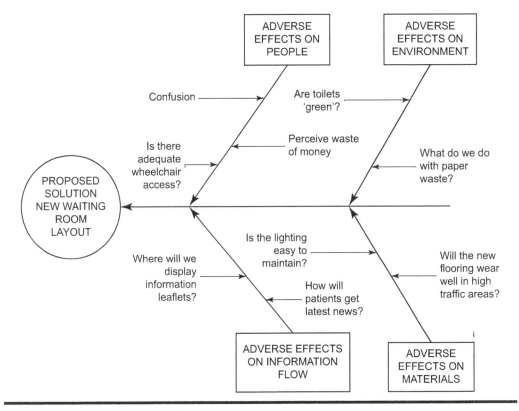

Figure 20.5   Solution effect diagram.

Method 11: The 2 × 2 Matrix

Type of problem that this method is useful for:

'We would like to understand the connections between empathy and competence'.

In Chapter 12, two matrices were used to explain different combinations of people's character.

The following one gives my own view of the relationship between empathy and competence.

The next stage would be to understand the position of the boundaries between high and low and how to manage these different people. Think of your workplace and try to position any extreme people you know. What safeguards would you put in pace to protect patients from types 1, 2 and 3? (Table 20.5).

Table 20.5   The Importance of Empathy in Healthcare

	Low Degree of Empathy ↓	*High Degree of Empathy* ↓
High Skill Level →	2 Skilled but poor 'bedside manner'. Needs 'chaperoning'.	4 The person everyone wants to go to.
Low Skill Level →	1 Not suited to healthcare.	3 Useful at limited number of tasks.

Method 12: Reflective Listening

Type of problem that this method is useful for:

'We need to be sure we have understood what was being said in our interviews'.

Reflective listening is a method of communication in which the questioner or investigator allows the person being questioned to explain his/her ideas, and then the questioner in his/her own words repeats back either exactly what has been said or the questioner's interpretation of what has been said. The person then has the opportunity to agree or disagree with either the statement or the interpretation.

Having reached agreement, the questioner or investigator can ask whether they can record the agreed interpretation in the notes of the meeting, reading out what is being written as it is written.

This method can be extremely useful in a situation where there is tension around the matter being discussed. The listening investigator does not express any opinions or emotions but calmly repeats what is being said.

The questioner will use phrases such as

- 'Are you telling me that ...'
- 'When you used the word "uncomfortable", what did you mean?'
- 'In recording what you are telling me, can I write ...?'

This method of questioning requires great self-control on behalf of the questioner not to get drawn into an evaluation of what is being said.

By being neutral like this, the questioner can gain the confidence of the person that they are really being listened to. Hopefully, it will avoid the situation where the subject comes back with 'No, you are not listening to what I am saying' or 'You don't understand me', even when the person is quite unintelligible.

Chapter 21

Selecting and Prioritising Improvement Projects

SUMMARY

It is better to have a logical system for prioritising projects than to simply respond to the crisis of the moment.

Many businesses do not have a structured approach to solving the problems or issues that arise during 'Business as Usual' meetings. Instead, a willing hand is often delegated to investigate and come up with an answer; it could be you. The result is that the person adds new projects to his/her list, and depending on how pressing their normal job is, the time to work on it will be 'whenever I get a chance'.

There was an example of a frustrated operations manager who, after a monthly management meeting, said, 'I now have Improvement Actions numbers 27, 28 and 29 on top of the 26 I already have!' The director handed these out like confetti.

On the other hand, a good manager will be in control of the situation, as in the case of a senior manager who once said, 'If I catch anyone working on anything we have not agreed to, they will have me to answer to!' A logical structured and documented approach is necessary.

Suppose you are working in a medium-size community healthcare centre with about 100 employees. At the moment, there are eight possible projects that are ongoing, shown in Table 21.1. You have limited resources, and due to staff cutbacks you need to review the list to give more priority to some projects than to others. In addition, there have been changes to the contract, and certain new projects must be started. How do you approach this problem?

Concentrate on What Matters, Ignore the Least Beneficial

It follows that a method is needed to decide which topics to tackle first. Indeed, it is also important to agree which topics to ignore, to concentrate only on what was agreed as the most important. The aim of this exercise is to score problems to help management produce a ranking table, most important to least important.

Because there are so many different healthcare organisations and systems, a book like this can only give the reader ideas from which to develop their own methods. The importance of methods such as these can show the openness, transparency and auditability of the whole scheme of improvement.

Take each project in turn, and ask the following questions A to H in Table 21.2.

Justification

From questions such as those listed previously, a justification for the project can be prepared that will give very rough estimates of the benefits of the work.

A quantitative value will be generated for each project, the project total points ranging from 0 = poor to 14 = good, and an estimate of the financial benefit, where relevant. This statement can be documented and distributed to the operational management team for information, debate and the preparation of the terms of reference.

Table 21.2 shows the justification for the project.

Ranking

The result or deliverable of this method will be a project list, which is ranked for ability to achieve benefits. If the aforementioned scoring system does not give a clear result, then many companies resort to a voting system.

Table 21.1   Ongoing Continuous Improvement Projects

Ref.	Project Title	Project Theme	Project Objective (Quantified)
1	Training	Increase number of nurses to have master's qualification	100% of nurses to be qualified to master's level
2	Anti-virus programme	Reduce number of viruses, install improved anti-virus and firewall	All desk PCs and laptops protected all day every day
3	Waiting times	Reduce waiting times in X area	No patient to wait for more than 20 minutes after appointment time
4	Dispensary A	Reduce number of customer complaints	Less than one in 3 months
5	Dispensary B	Reduce the number of delayed prescriptions	Less than one per week
6	Online booking system	Increase data handling capacity of IT system, upgrade	New server +12 terminals
7	Faster comms	Reduce communication times, provide all community nurses with tablet PCs	Eight new tablet PCs to provide immediate connection to server all day every day
8	Call handling	Increase the call handling capacity	Twenty calls simultaneously with 5-second maximum response

Voting Method

In the voting method the list of projects is given to the management team; each member can allocate three points for their first choice, two to their second and first to their third. The highest scoring projects are chosen for development work.

Table 21.2 Relative Scoring System for Improvement Ideas/Projects

Project Ref.				
Project Title				
Project Theme				
A	Do we have enough data to start immediately?	Yes/No	Yes = 1	
B	Is a feasibility study needed?	Yes/No	No = 1	
C	Do we have the skills to develop this improvement ourselves?	Yes/No	Yes = 1	
D	What will the benefits be: Large or small? Quantify if possible.		Large = 1	
E	Will any benefits be immediate (weeks)?	Yes/No	Yes = 1	
F	Will the benefit(s) have an immediate (months) positive impact on a patient safety score? What score would that be?	Yes/No	Yes = 1	
G	Does the cost fit within our budget?	Yes/No	Yes = 1	
H	Is it obligatory to fulfil our contract?	Yes/No	Yes = 7	
	Total points	Max	14	

No One Knows Any Better than This

If at some time in the future someone suggests that the wrong projects were chosen, remember they were the best that the best brains in the organisation could think of at the time.

Chapter 22

Multiple Project Management

SUMMARY

Having a formal project management approach will increase the chances of succeeding. It will also demonstrate to external inspectors that a structured, focused programme of improvement is in place.

Imagine being at an operational management meeting and in front of everyone is a list of all the ideas for improving the organisation; those ideas being worked on, those completed and those yet to start. No one can dispute what is or is not on the list, and if they do not agree, the list can be corrected and priorities can be changed. This is a very desirable state to be in, but how do you reach that position? Let's call it a continuous improvement (CI) register.

The Continuous Improvement Register

CI registers can take as many formats as there are businesses using them, but there will be some basic fields or column headings common to most. The term 'field' is used here because of the opportunity at some stage to put the information into an electronic database.

Consistency of Thought, Terminology and Presentation

A frequently occurring factor which inhibits smooth progress on improvement projects is a slack attitude and indiscipline towards the terminology used. I have seen and heard it many times. For example, the aim of the project should be expressed the same way every time it is discussed or presented. This leads to a common focus on the shared objectives.

If during the course of the project the recognised or standard terminology is challenged, for example for being too vague or inaccurate, then the standard documented statement should be 'officially revised'. By using the term officially revised I am referring to standard document control rules which should be applied to all project documentation. These rules include

- Each controlled document is given a unique reference number.
- The structure of any document cannot be changed without approval. (Obviously forms can be filled in, this applies to the structure of the form.)
- Details are recorded in a change register of changes made to the project.
- Previous versions of documents are withdrawn from the system, such as old-style forms or out-of-date standard letters. Just compare this to telephone directories with out-of-date numbers.

Using this standardisation approach has the added benefit that an electronic database of the various terms can be used to produce interim or stage reports containing the standard terminology; it sounds boring, but it is effective!

Document Control

Many people do not understand the importance of document control, especially when it applies to say 'standard letters'.

I have come across this myself with letters sent to me telling me of an appointment. This particular letter included instructions that no longer applied to the appointment process I was to participate in. As a consequence, when I telephoned to clarify what I should do, I was told that a paragraph in the letter was no longer relevant and I should ignore it. When I told the helper on the other end of the phone that a new standard letter should be created, I was told that it could not be done. They did not have the authority to change the letter. That standard letter was out of date and should have been withdrawn.

The Analytical Process

Creating the CI register is also the start of the analytical process to understand the ideas being discussed. Each of the column headings suggested here will be carried forward throughout the project, using the standardised words every time, as if they were created by a rubber stamp or in information technology terms, 'copy and paste'. This is for the accuracy and consistency described already. The clearer the terminology, the more focused the team will be.

Revised Ideas and Changes

Very often, midway through a project the team discovers that their early assumptions were incorrect, ambiguous or too broad and have to be changed. This is good. The change can be made in a controlled fashion, and the tool to use for this is shown in Table 22.1.

The CI register will eventually look like the table shown in Figure 22.1, but at first there might only be entries in columns 2 and 3 because evaluation, justification and feasibility will not have been carried out. At this stage they are only ideas.

These headings should be interpreted as shown in Table 22.2; the final statement used in each cell of the register will become the standard words and numbers used throughout all of the stages of the project, unless a conscious decision is made to deliberately change the team's aims, assumptions or conclusions (as described previously).

An example of typical entries in a CI register was shown in Table 21.1 (columns 1, 2 and 3 only). It is best prepared in Microsoft Excel, and when changes are made, say each month, the spreadsheet should be saved as a new version – do not overwrite old files. This way audit traceability can be achieved. (The audit would be necessary for Care Quality Commission inspections or ISO 9001 Quality Standard.)

Table 22.1   CI Project Register

1	2	3	4	5	6	7	8	9
Ref.	Project Title	Project Theme	Project Objective (Quantified)	Sponsor	Project Leader	Status/ Priority	Target Completion Date	Progress Reviewed At
1								
2								
3								
4								

Table 22.2 Standard Project Terminology

Column	Field name	Description
1	Ref.	The sequential number given to the project.
2	Project title	A catchy nickname for the project, containing several unique/memorable words.
3	Project theme	Something very descriptive, ideally starting with 'reducing' or 'increasing'.
4	Project objective	A numerical target, impacting on a healthcare statistic that can be measured. An objective must be SMART: S pecific, M easured, A greed, R ealistic, T imed
5	Project sponsor	A director who will take overall responsibility for the achievements of the development team.
6	Project leader	The person who leads the cross-functional improvement team.
7	Priority/status	Status can be one of 'not started', 'active' or 'completed'. Priority for projects not started is denoted as a ranked score from 1 to x.
8	Target completion date	Must be realistic.
9	Progress reviewed at	Choose from • Monthly senior management • Meetings • Weekly management • Meetings • Weekly departmental • Meetings • Daily departmental meetings

Use of the CI Register Following an External Inspection

Supposing your organisation has had an improvement notice from an external inspection organisation, then every item of improvement that the inspection team has reported must go into this project register. That way it provides a visible control plan until completed, and an auditable trail after completion.

Epilogue

Jennifer is now recovering thanks to some expert surgery, but her experiences raise many issues too numerous to list here. Each of those issues would lend itself to separate cause and effect analysis, but the overriding factors would question management and supervision standards at all levels and the feeling, not unjustified, 'This is the way it is. We are underfunded, understaffed and overworked, and we are doing our best, sorry'.

What is needed in that particular hospital is much better leadership at all levels and many more inspiring role models.

This story is for just one patient out of 1 million treated nationally every 36 hours[1]; within one hospital out of about 1500; having an operation, just one of 10 million surgical procedures a year, in a world-leading health service.

Jennifer believes that had her condition been diagnosed more quickly, and had she had better aftercare, she could have been discharged several days earlier. In the report 'Exploring the costs of unsafe care in the NHS', October 2014, by Frontier Economics Europe,[2] Section 2.2 states the Health and Social Care Information Centre as estimating the cost of an inpatient stay at £3,366 per day, as well as denying another patient treatment. When working in organisations in which errors are occurring, I have heard the statement many times that 'we haven't time to make improvements'. However, to correct those mistakes the organisation has to find the time to do the work again, usually at a higher cost than if they had got it 'Right First Time'. They couldn't really afford not to make changes.

Is Jennifer's Tale typical or exceptional?

References

Preface

1. The Mid Staffordshire NHS Foundation Trust Public Inquiry; The Francis Report. 2013.
2. Campbell, D. Mid Staffs hospital scandal: The essential guide. *The Guardian*, 2013. https://www.theguardian.com/society/2013/feb/06/mid-staffs-hospital-scandal-guide.
3. The report of the Morecambe Bay Investigation; the Kirkup Report. 2015.
4. Campbell, D. Jeremy Hunt orders investigation into baby deaths at NHS trust. *The Guardian*, 2017. https://www.theguardian.com/society/2017/apr/12/jeremy-hunt-orders-investigation-into-baby-deaths-at-nhs-trust.
5. Perraudin, F. Police investigating baby deaths at Countess of Chester hospital. *The Guardian*, 2017. https://www.theguardian.com/uk-news/2017/may/18/police-investigating-baby-deaths-at-countess-of-chester-hospital.
6. Nebehay, S. Going into hospital far riskier than flying: WHO. *Reuters Health News*, 21 July 2011.
7. James, J. T. A new evidence based estimate of patient harms associated with hospital care. *Journal of Patient Safety*, 2013; 9(3): 122–128.
8. Makary, M. A. and Daniel, M.. Medical error – the third leading cause of death in the US. *BMJ*, 2016; 353: i2139.

Chapter One

1. Bird, F. E. Director of Engineering Services for the Insurance Company of North America (INA). 1969.
2. Heinrich, H. W. *Industrial Accident Prevention, a Scientific Approach.* McGraw-Hill. 1931.
3. Reason, J. The contribution of latent human failures to the breakdown of complex systems. *Philosophical Transactions of the Royal Society of London. Series B, Biological Sciences*, 1990; 327(1241): 475–484.
4. Syed, M. *Black Box Thinking.* John Murray, London. 2015.

Chapter Two

1. NHS Resolution; Business Plan 2017/18. http://www.nhsla.com/AboutUs/Documents/NHS%20Resolution%20-%20%20Business%20Plan%202017-18.pdf.
2. NHS Litigation Authority. http://resolution.nhs.uk/about. 2017.
3. NHS Confederation; Key statistics on the NHS. 2016. http://www.nhsconfed.org/resources/key-statistics-on-the-nhs.
4. The Medical Protection Society. https://www.medicalprotection.org/uk/for-members/press-releases/press-releases/clinical-negligence-costs-at-tipping-point---urgent-reform-needed.
5. Office of National Statistics; Birth summary tables – England and Wales. https://www.ons.gov.uk/peoplepopulationandcommunity/birthsdeathsandmarriages/livebirths/datasets/birthsummarytables. 2009.
6. Mello, M. M., Chandra, A., Gawande, A. A. and Studdert, D. M. National costs of the medical liability system. *Health Aff*, 2010, 29(9): 1569–1577.
7. The Mid Staffordshire NHS Foundation Trust Public Inquiry; the Francis Report. 2013.
8. Improving the safety of patients in England; the Berwick Report. 2013.
9. The report of the Morecambe Bay Investigation; the Kirkup Report. 2015.
10. Sands Stillbirth and Neonatal Death Charity. https://www.sands.org.uk/key-facts. 2017.
11. Office of National Statistics; Birth summary tables – England and Wales. https://www.ons.gov.uk/peoplepopulationandcommunity/birthsdeathsandmarriages/livebirths/datasets/birthsummarytables. 2014.
12. Flenady, V., et al. Stillbirths: Recall to action in high-income countries. *The Lancet*, 2016, 387(10019): 691–702. http://www.thelancet.com/action/showFullTextImages?pii=S0140-6736%2815%2901020-X.
13. Manktelow, B. N., Smith, L. K., Seaton, S. E., Hyman-Taylor, P., Kurinczuk, J. J., Field, D. J., Smith, P. W., and Draper, E. S. MBRRACE-UK. Perinatal mortality surveillance report. May 2016.
14. Briggs, T. Getting it right first time; British Orthopaedic Association. Stanmore, Middlesex, 2012.
15. Care Quality Commission. The state of health care and adult social care in England 2014/15. 2015.
16. NHS Safety Thermometer: National report 2012–2014. 2014. http://harmfreecare.org/wp-content/files_mf/NHS-Safety-Thermometer-National-Report.pdf.
17. National Safety Thermometer 2014–2016: Patient harms and harm free care. 2016.

Chapter Three

1. NHS England, The never events list 2013/2014 Update. 2013. https://www.england.nhs.uk/wp-content/uploads/2013/12/nev-ev-list-1314-clar.pdf.

2. Patients Association press release, Patients association calls for 'never' incidents to cease. http://www.patients-association.org.uk/wp-content/uploads/2016/02/press-release-call-for-never-incidents-to-cease.pdf. 2016.
3. NHS Confederation, Key statistics on the NHS. 2016. http://www.nhsconfed.org/resources/key-statistics-on-the-nhs.
4. National Safety Thermometer 2014–2016: Patient harms and harm free care. 2016.
5. Alexander, R. Which is the world's biggest employer? BBC. 2012. http://www.bbc.co.uk/news/magazine-17429786.

Chapter Four

1. Jan Carlzon Quotes, azquotes. http://www.azquotes.com/quote/549093.
2. RCN Guidelines: Perioperative fasting in adults and children. November 2005.

Chapter Five

1. BBC, Apeman – Spaceman. *Human Universe*. 2014. http://www.bbc.co.uk/programmes/p0276pc3.
2. Deming, W. E. *Out of the Crisis*. Cambridge, MA, MIT Press. 1986.

Chapter Six

1. Care Quality Commission; Hospitals. http://www.cqc.org.uk/content/hospitals.
2. NHS Confederation; NHS statistics, facts and figures. http://www.nhsconfed.org/resources/key-statistics-on-the-nhs. London. 2016.
3. NHS Choices; The NHS in England. http://www.nhs.uk/NHSEngland/thenhs/about/Pages/overview.aspx.
4. From a blame culture to a learning culture; Health Secretary addresses the Global Patient Safety Summit on improving safety standards in healthcare. Department of Health, London, 2016.

Chapter Seven

1. American Society for Quality; Quality glossary – Q. https://asq.org/quality-resources/quality-glossary/q. Milwaukee. 2017.
2. Chartered Quality Institute; CQI grade quiz. https://www.quality.org/article/what-quality. 2017.
3. The Lord Darzi of Denham; Department of Health; Our NHS, our future; interim report. 2007.

4. The Lord Darzi of Denham; Department of Health; High quality care for all: NHS Next Stage Review, final report. 2008.
5. International Organization for Standardization ISO 9001:2015 Quality management systems; Requirements; Geneva. 2015.
6. National Safety Thermometer 2014–2016: Patient harms and harm free care. 2016.
7. The King's Fund; The number of hospital beds. https://www.kingsfund.org.uk/projects/nhs-in-a-nutshell/hospital-beds. 2017.
8. Dame Janet Smith DBE, *The Shipman Enquiry; First Report*, July 2002.
9. Care Quality Commission; The state of care in acute NHS hospitals 2014–2016. February 2017.
10. Imai, M. *Kaizen: The Key to Japan's Competitive Success*. New York, Random House. 1986.
11. Kenney, C. *A Leadership Journey in Health Care: Virginia Mason's Story*. Boca Raton, FL, Productivity Press. 2015.
12. Langton, D. J., Sidaginamele, R. P., Avery, P., et al. Retrospective cohort study of the performance of the Pinnacle metal on metal (MoM) total hip replacement: a single-centre investigation in combination with the findings of a national retrieval centre. *BMJ Open*, 2016: 6:e007847. doi:10.1136/bmjopen-2015-007847.

Chapter Eight

1. Care Quality Commission. The state of health care and adult social care in England 2014/15. 2015.
2. Barlow, J. and Moller, C.. *A Complaint Is a Gift*. Oakland, CA, Berrett-Koehler Publishers. 1996.
3. Warden, J. Mrs Bottomley defends doctors. *BMJ*, 1993, 307: 88. http://www.bmj.com/content/bmj/307/6896/88.full.pdf.
4. NHS England, NHS England complaints policy. September 2014.
5. UK Patients Association, Good practice standards for NHS complaints handling. September 2013.

Chapter Nine

1. British Standards, BS 7850 Part 2; 1992. Withdrawn. B.S.I. Group, London.
2. Groocock, J. B. *The Chain of Quality: Market Dominance through Product Superiority*. Wiley; London. 1986.

Chapter Ten

1. Briggs, T. Getting it right first time; British Orthopaedic Association. Stanmore, Middlesex, 2012.

Chapter Eleven

1. Vincent, C. *Patient Safety*. London, Elsevier. 2006.
2. Hayakawa, S.I. *Language in Thought and Action*. New York, Harcourt Inc. 1990.
3. Korzybski, A. *Science and Sanity: An Introduction to Non-Aristotelian Systems and General Semantics*; 5th edn. Englewood, NJ, Institute of General Semantics. 1995.

Chapter Twelve

1. NHS England; *Policy Book for Primary Medical Services*. 2016. https://www.england.nhs.uk/commissioning/wp-content/uploads/sites/12/2016/01/policy-book-pms.pdf, p. 5.

Chapter Fourteen

1. NHS; National Patient Safety Agency. http://www.nrls.npsa.nhs.uk/home/.
2. Care Quality Commission; Nigel's surgery. http://www.cqc.org.uk/guidance-providers/gp-services/nigels-surgery-3-significant-event-analysis-sea.
3. Jones, R. V. *Most Secret War*. London, Coronet Books. 1990.
4. Delivering the NHS Safety Thermometer CQUIN 2012/135; NHS Safety Thermometer National Report 2012–2014. 2014. http://harmfreecare.org/wp-content/files_mf/NHS-Safety-Thermometer-National-Report.pdf.
5. National Safety Thermometer 2014–2016, Patient harms and harm free care. 2016.

Chapter Fifteen

1. Dame Janet Smith DBE, *The Shipman Enquiry; First Report*, July 2002.

Chapter Sixteen

1. Maternity Deaths. Various, including http://www.ons.gov.uk/ons/guide-method/user-guidance/health-and-life-events/index.html; https://www.sands.org.uk/our-work/baby-death-current-picture/why-babies-die; http://www.1000livesplus.wales.nhs.uk/home.

Chapter Eighteen

1. Carey, R. G. and Lloyd, R. C. *Measuring Quality Improvement in Healthcare.* ASQ, Milwaukee. 2001.
2. Vincent, C. *Patient Safety.* London, Elsevier. 2006.
3. The Hawthorne effect. *The Economist.* http://www.economist.com/node/12510632. 2008.

Epilogue

1. NHS Choices. The NHS in England. http://www.nhs.uk/NHSEngland/thenhs/about/Pages/overview.aspx. 2017.
2. Exploring the costs of unsafe care in the NHS; October 2014. London, Frontier Economics Europe. 2014.

Background Reading

An organisation with a memory; the Donaldson Report. 2000

Quality governance in the NHS; National Quality Board. 2011.

Quality improvement made simple; the Health Foundation. 2013.

NHS Health Check programme standards: A framework for quality improvement; Public Health England. 2014.

Exploring the costs of unsafe care in the NHS; October 2014. London, Frontier Economics LTD. 2014.

Lloyd P. Provost and Sandra Murray; *The Health Care Data Guide: Learning from Data for Improvement*; San Francisco, CA; Jossey-Bass; 2011.

Charles Vincent; *Patient Safety*; London; Elsevier Churchill Livingstone; 2006.

Gerald L. Langley, Ronald D. Moen, Kevin M. Nolan, Thomas W. Nolan, Clifford L. Norman, Lloyd P. Provost; *The Improvement Guide: A Practical Approach to Enhancing Organizational Performance*; San Francisco, CA; Jossey-Bass; 2009.

Robert C. Lloyd and Raymond G. Carey; *Measuring Quality Improvement in Healthcare: A Guide to Statistical Process Control Applications*; Milwaukee, WI; ASQ; 2000.

Masaaki Imai; *Kaizen: The Key to Japan's Competitive Success*; New York; Random House; 1986.

Index